I0427884

Table of Contents

The Role of Congress in the Strategic Posture of the United States, 1942-1960: Manhattan Project to the New Look

Introduction

This is the fourth in a series of papers to examine the role of Congress in the development of the doctrinal and material strategic posture of the United States. Previous papers examined the role of Congress in building the U.S. strategic posture during the decades of the 1960s, 1970s, and 1980s. This paper examines the role of the 77th-86th Congresses, from 1942 to 1960, an eighteen year period that begins with the development of the first atomic weapons during the Manhattan Project and runs through the administration of President Dwight Eisenhower and the development of the "New Look" nuclear strategy.

The role of Congress in the development of the U.S. strategic posture is underappreciated by historians and policymakers. Histories of U.S. nuclear strategy and the weapons programs funded to implement that strategy typically focus on the executive branch, the Department of Defense, the military services, and academic theorists as the prime movers. Indeed, at least one historical treatment describes the role of Congress in the development of the U.S. strategic posture as merely a passive "rubberstamp" for the Department of Defense, not only on matters of doctrine and weapons programs, but even on "oversight responsibilities with regard to the nuclear weapons budget."[1]

In fact, Congress played an important, often dominant, role in the development of U.S. doctrine and nuclear forces that are the basis of the strategic posture of the United States. Moreover, the congressional record is a rich resource, not least for being unclassified, that documents the important role of Congress in strategic matters. The congressional record provides often meticulous detail on the debates and thinking of congressional, administration, military service, and academic actors on the evolution of the strategic posture. Yet this resource is underutilized by historians, which may account in part for their underestimation of the importance of the role Congress has in this area. The paper draws heavily from the congressional record, letting the actors speak for themselves as much as possible, to demonstrate the richness of this neglected resource, to encourage further research, and because it is the best way to tell the story.

This paper presents a very brief history on the role of Congress in making the U.S. strategic posture during the seminal period 1942-1960, when atomic and nuclear weapons and their delivery systems were new and rapidly evolving technologies. It treats the highlights of this period when the foundations of the U.S. strategic posture were undergoing material and intellectual creation.

As Congress and its role in the development of the strategic posture is the subject of this paper, the focus shall be on the Congress, and not on the President, the Department of Defense, the military services, or academic theorists. The roles of these actors are the usual subjects of histories of nuclear strategy and the strategic posture, and have already been exhaustively analyzed elsewhere. Moreover, this is not a history of specific bomber and missile programs. Although Congress certainly influences and often plays a decisive role in such programs, its impact on these programs does not represent the largest contributions Congress makes to the development of the strategic posture.

The paper treats a period now a half century in the past. Yet this period arguably is the most important and most interesting in the series. The years 1942-1960 were innovative decades that saw the invention of atomic weapons and their integration into U.S. national security strategy and policy. The lessons to be learned from this challenging period may be in many respects the most relevant for present or future policymakers confronted, or gifted, with a revolutionary new military technology that must be harnessed and integrated with strategic doctrine and military operational plans in order to advance the national security and geopolitical objectives of the United States.

The Manhattan Project

One common historical myth is that Congress played no role in the Manhattan Project that developed the first atomic bombs. For example, according to an article in the *Bulletin of the Atomic Scientists*, "Congress was not informed" of the Manhattan Project.[2] Even Richard Rhodes' otherwise excellent book on the Manhattan Project, *The Making of the Atomic Bomb*, considered by some scholars to be a definitive and exhaustive history, barely mentions the role of Congress in the Project.[3]

Yet the Manhattan Project would not have been possible without the help of Congress. Just as knowledge of the atomic bomb program was very limited in the executive branch, knowledge of the Manhattan Project within the congressional branch was limited to only a few members. Secrecy surrounding the Manhattan Project necessitated abandoning the normal mechanisms of executive and congressional oversight and led to changing the rules that normally governed military programs.

Originally driven by the fear that Nazi Germany might be ahead in the race for an atomic bomb, the Manhattan Project gave birth to the "culture of secrecy" that dominated the atomic bomb program, a culture that continued to dominate atomic and nuclear weapons programs after World War II. Leaks in the U.S. A-bomb program could enable Germany to develop atomic weapons first, or so it was feared at the time.

As early as January 1939, Leo Szilard and other physicists exploring the possibility of atomic weapons imposed self-censorship on their nucleonics research after Germany became the first nation to achieve a nuclear chain reaction. The "culture of secrecy" continued after the U.S. government established the Uranium Committee, which investigated the technological feasibility of an atomic bomb.[4]

Even the Uranium Committee, this first early step toward the Manhattan Project, was made possible by the Congress, albeit without congressional knowledge at this time. The Uranium Committee and its relatively modest needs was concealed within and supported by the Bureau of Standards, established by an Act of Congress in 1901, and charged with applying science and technology for the national interest. The Bureau of Standards became the nation's tiny physics lab and a natural home for the Uranium Committee.[5]

The work investigating the feasibility of the A-bomb accomplished under the auspices of the Uranium Committee evolved to become the Manhattan Project, the program to build an atomic bomb, and the "culture of secrecy" expanded dramatically from a few dozen scientists to encompass hundreds of thousands of workers. General Leslie Groves, director of the Manhattan Project, introduced "compartmentalization" so that working groups focused on narrow technological problems, their work kept secret from other working groups to safeguard against espionage and leaks. Groves introduced the principle that all nuclear research is "born classified."[6]

The Manhattan Project "culture of secrecy" created and encompassed entire cities. For example, at Oak Ridge, Tennessee, the U.S. government--without explanation to the residents or the state governor--took over thousands of acres of farmland, expelling over 1,000 inhabitants, giving them $34 an acre and three weeks to vacate their homes. Within months, a "secret city" of 75,000 workers and their families, along with laboratories and vast industrial facilities to work on fuel for the atomic bomb, arose on what had been fields of rural farmland. Outsiders were not permitted to visit Oak Ridge, or other "secret cities" like it, all of which had become part of the Manhattan Project. Workers were told not to discuss their jobs with one another or with family members.[7]

Clearly, this "culture of secrecy" was incompatible with the normal and highly public processes of executive and congressional oversight applied to normal military programs.

In the White House, President Franklin Roosevelt, Secretary of War Henry Stimson, and General George C. Marshall were privy to the Manhattan Project's secrets. There were others of the executive branch who knew about the Manhattan Project, like Dr. Vannevar Bush, who worked actively on and within the Project.

Even the Vice President was ignorant of the Manhattan Project, until Vice President Truman had to succeed the deceased Roosevelt, when Truman was briefed by Stimson.[8]

In the House of Representatives, House Speaker Sam Rayburn, Majority Leader John W. McCormack, and Minority Leader Joseph W. Martin, like President Roosevelt, were privy to the secrets of the Manhattan Project. In the U.S. Senate, privy to the Manhattan Project were Majority Leader Alben W. Barkley, Minority Leader Wallace H. White, Chairman of the Military Appropriations Subcommittee Elmer Thomas, and Ranking Member of that subcommittee, Senator Styles Bridges. All were briefed by Secretary of War Stimson, General Marshall, and Dr. Bush.[9]

In 1962, retired Army General Leslie Groves, who had been director of the Manhattan Project, described a detailed briefing given to House leaders that included not just the Project's funding requirements, but also the scientific background and military potential of atomic weapons. Congressmen Rayburn, McCormack, and Martin agreed to finance the Manhattan Project and keep the project secret from other House members. Groves:

> Mr. Stimson reviewed the general state of the project and discussed the financial situation, including expenditures, available monies and estimated future requirements. He gave them our general program of construction, talked of the various possible procurement efforts and indicated an approximate schedule for the completion of our work. General Marshall talked of the project's relation to America's over-all strategic war plans, and Bush outlined the scientific background and explained the potentialities of the weapon.

> The Congressmen indicated their approval without reservation. They said that, while the amount of money needed was large, they were in full agreement that the expenditures were justified, and they would do everything possible to have the necessary funds included in the upcoming Appropriations Bill. It would not be necessary, they said, to make any further explanations to the Appropriations Committee.[10]

Congressional leaders like Rayburn, McCormack, Martin and their Senate colleagues made the Manhattan Project possible and played an indispensable role in keeping it secret by finding ways to discretely fund research and development of the atomic bomb. They hid the Manhattan Project in the U.S. Army budget. The stature of these leaders was so great among members of Congress that they could direct Appropriations Committee and Subcommittee chairmen to "look the other way" and not ask revealing questions of mysterious line items that were funding parts of the A-bomb program. In 1947, Senator Millard Tydings remembered this "no questions" approach to funding the Manhattan Project:

> General Marshall came before the Appropriations Committee one day and said in effect this: "Gentlemen, I want you to give me a billion dollars. I do not want you to ask me what it is going to be used for. It is a military secret, but I hope you will give me the money. The Committee responded by asking whether a billion dollars would be enough.[11]

Manhattan Project director Groves gives some sense of the monumental debt owed to the success of the Manhattan Project to a handful of House and Senate congressional leaders, just seven in all, who shouldered the responsibility for overseeing the appropriation of the Project's multi-

billion dollar budget, using their personal influence to preserve the Project's secrecy. Groves:

> During the early days, because of our rapidly changing plans, it had not been possible to establish any regular budgeting procedures. We were allocated funds that were already available to the War Department on an "as required" basis. For Fiscal Years 1945 and 1946 [calendar years 1944 and 1945], however, we had to ask for new funds. These requests were concealed in other requests for appropriations. During the entire period, we were allocated approximately $2,300,000,000 of which $2,191,000,000 were expended through December 31, 1946....

> Before July 1, 1945, a majority of our money came from two sources--Engineer Service, Army; and Expediting Production...In justifying our requests for these funds, we were handicapped not only by the very size of the project and its many uncertainties, which made it impossible to budget in advance, but by the overriding need for secrecy, in the spending as well as in the getting....

> It was agreed at this time that [House Speaker] Rayburn would be given advance notice of how our requests for appropriations would be inserted in the bill. He would pass this information on to [House Majority Leader] McCormack and [House Minority Leader] Martin, and the three of them would tell a few members of the Appropriations Committee that they had gone into the subject with Secretary Stimson and General Marshall and that these items should not be questioned. The other members of Congress would be given only the most general reasons for the need to accord special handling to our requests for funds.[12]

Senator Harry Truman, before he became Vice President, proved to be an exception in

this pattern of acquiescence to the influence of such leaders as Rayburn, McCormack, and

Martin. As Chairman of the Committee to Investigate the National Defense Program, Senator

Truman started an investigation that threatened to expose the Manhattan Project. However,

intervention by Secretary Stimson persuaded Truman to abandon his inquiry until after the war.[13]

During the war, the executive branch and the military were sensitive to the constitutional

powers of the Congress and the necessity of congressional cooperation to provide funding for the

Manhattan Project. For example, prior to the Manhattan Project, the administration considered

the formation of a Military Policy Committee that would have put Congress in charge of the

Project. But this was rejected in favor of running the Manhattan Project through the U.S. Army

Corps of Engineers. In October 1944, Vannevar Bush and James B. Conant persuaded Secretary

of War Stimson to establish the Harvey-Bundy Interim Committee, to make legislative

recommendations on nuclear weapons to the post-war Congress.[14] This move recognized that

the way the Manhattan Project was run during the exceptional circumstances of World War II

could not continue afterwards, that Congress would have to be more fully informed about the

atomic weapons program, and that the Congress would have to reassert its normal oversight

powers. In this connection, the Smyth Report was prepared and provided to Congress on August

12, 1945, just days after the Hiroshima and Nagasaki atomic bombings, as a declassified primer

on the Manhattan Project.[15]

Manhattan Project leader and scientist Vannevar Bush, writing in his 1949 book *Modern

Arms and Free Men*, represented the predominant view of the executive branch and the military

services on the crucial role of Congress in helping build the intellectual and material foundations

of a national security policy incorporating the new technology of atomic weapons:

> There are military experts in Congress. Certainly there are, just as there are many
> experts in law, a few professors, and even a few highly competent engineers.
> These men are particularly valuable, and those who have had military experience
> and who are close students of military history, strategy, or tactics are especially
> valuable in the examination of whether the military organization is running
> well....The President, through his subordinates to whom he delegates authority,
> will have the primary duty of seeing to it that the system is well manned and
> performing well. But Congress can look in and check, as indeed is its prerogative
> and duty, and every member of Congress who is charged with so doing by his
> assignments can participate, and he does not need to be a specialist in order to do
> so.
>
> It will be well to pause and examine this last point further, for it is at the heart of
> the success of much of our democratic process. How does it happen that a
> Congressman who was a small-town lawyer in private life can sit on a committee
> and judge wisely whether the military organization is running well, whether its
> proposals appear sound, and whether its appropriations should be cut or extended?

Congress is composed of successful politicians. To be successful as a politician a man needs many talents...Especially he needs one attribute: the ability to judge men, the ability above all to know whom he can trust. Without that quality he does not get to Congress....How did Congress decide during the war to throw billions into the race for the atomic bomb? Because there were leaders of Congress who had the confidence of their fellows and because those leaders trusted the elder statesman who was then Secretary of War, Henry L. Stimson.[16]

Could a modern day Manhattan Project--a project requiring vast national resources, including the construction of "secret cities," to create a revolution in science and military weapons--succeed and achieve similarly monumental goals in secret?

The circumstances of the Manhattan Project were no doubt historically unique. Patriotism trumped partisan feeling in the aftermath of Pearl Harbor. The clear threat from military dictatorships to the very existence of the Western Democracies led citizens and political leaders alike to subordinate self-interest to the national interest with unprecedented enthusiasm. Congressional members trusted and deferred to leaders of Congress on funding and preserving the secrecy of the Manhattan Project. Congressional leaders did their part for the Manhattan Project in no small measure because of personal respect and deference to Secretary of War Stimson. One could argue that the heightened partisanship of U.S. political culture today would make it impossible to achieve the degree of unity and trust necessary to sustain a modern version of the Manhattan Project, even in the face of an equally grave threat.

Whatever the prospects for a future Manhattan Project may be, even the Manhattan Project of World War II cannot be considered a complete success. Importantly for the decades after 1945, the Manhattan Project, despite all of its "culture of secrecy," failed to protect the secret of the atomic bomb. Germany and Japan were kept in the dark. But the Soviet Union penetrated the Manhattan Project. Soviet atomic spies enabled Moscow, unknown to Washington, to launch its own crash program to develop nuclear weapons. Ironically, the Smyth

Report, the first official unclassified publication on atomic energy, supposedly crafted to avoid disclosing secrets, helped the Soviet atomic bomb isotope separation program.[17] With the shock of the Red A-bomb detonation of 1949, the USSR quickly put an end to the U.S. "atomic monopoly" and posed an unprecedented nuclear challenge to the entire West.

Atomic Infrastructure and Institutions

With amazing alacrity and within a matter of months after the Hiroshima and Nagasaki atomic bombings, Congress reasserted its traditional powers and oversight role to manage the scientific-military revolution represented by the invention of the A-bomb and the emergence of peaceful use of nuclear energy. Between 1945 and 1947, Congress established the scientific laboratories and defense-industrial base that became the technological and manufacturing sinews of the U.S. strategic posture for decades to come. During this same period and within two years after Nagasaki, Congress forged the institutional framework to guide and govern the intellectual and doctrinal development of U.S. atomic and overall military strategy and integrate the revolutionary new technology represented by atomic weapons into the national security policy of the United States. Congress created by 1947 most of the national security establishment familiar to us today--the Department of Defense, the Joint Chiefs of Staff, the military services, the National Security Council, and the Central Intelligence Agency--and once vitally important institutions that may no longer be so familiar, such as the Atomic Energy Commission, the Special Committee on Atomic Energy, and the Joint Committee on Atomic Energy.

History oftentimes is misconstrued as marching inevitably to the present. But in the immediate aftermath of World War II, with Europe and Asia in ruins, the old world order shattered and a new world order still emerging, and all overshadowed by the threat and promise of atomic energy, everything was in doubt, including the future of atomic energy.

Where atomic weapons and energy were concerned, the Truman administration realized that, with World War II won, there were no guarantees that Congress would continue to support investing peacetime dollars into the atomic laboratories and industries. These could be demobilized and abandoned, along with the huge ground, sea, and air military forces that were rapidly disbanded after the war. Accordingly, the Truman administration, as noted earlier, provided the Smyth Report and proposed the establishment of an Atomic Energy Commission, to educate and sell Congress on the value of A-bombs and atomic energy and on the necessity of continuing to invest heavily in the related scientific-industrial infrastructure.

At the same time, the Truman administration's vision of the atomic future seemed contradictory and was controversial to many in Congress. If in the aftermath of World War II everything was in doubt, to the Truman administration everything also seemed possible, including building a new internationalist world order based partly on the promise of atomic energy. President Truman revived President Woodrow Wilson's vision of world peace through a League of Nations with the proposed establishment of the United Nations. Common wisdom and many historians argued that the original League of Nations failed to preserve world peace only because the United States followed a path of isolationism instead of world leadership through the League. The Truman administration saw the United Nations as an opportunity to rebuild the shattered world order on a peaceful basis, where national differences could be negotiated, and future world wars avoided.

As an inducement to the capitals of the world, including Moscow, to support the United Nations, the Truman administration proposed a peaceful atomic energy program to share technology internationally through the Baruch Plan. The Baruch Plan proposed that the United

Nations would control and regulate international access to atomic energy for peaceful uses,

making available to the world the promise of limitless energy as long as nations participating in

the plan pledged not to seek atomic weapons. The practical effect of the Baruch Plan intended

by most members of the Truman administration was to preserve the U.S. monopoly on atomic

weapons while creating a more pacific world order through a strong and meaningful United

Nations. However, at least some supporters of the Truman administration, notably J. Robert

Oppenheimer, the scientific leader of the Manhattan Project whose great influence continued

after World War II, were committed internationalists who did not want any nation, including the

United States, to have the A-bomb.

Congress as a whole was less enamored of the United Nations than the Truman

administration, more assertively nationalist in its orientation toward atomic energy, and much

more vocal in its determination to preserve the United States monopoly, and all the military and

political advantages to be accrued, from U.S. unilateral possession of the atomic bomb. The

actual policy differences between the Truman administration and the Congress over preserving

the U.S. monopoly on atomic weapons may have been more rhetorical than real. Nonetheless,

the differences in rhetoric and perception were enough to raise significant tensions between

Congress and the Truman administration over the years and spur more aggressive and more

robust institutional oversight by Congress.

Against this background, two months after the atomic bombing of Nagasaki, the

Congress took the first major step toward building the post-war atomic weapons infrastructure

with a hearing before the House Committee on Military Affairs on House Resolution 4280, "An

Act for the Development and Control of Atomic Energy." This was a proposal from the Truman administration to establish an Atomic Energy Commission (AEC) to continue the scientific-industrial project previously known as the Manhattan Project, but now to be managed differently, as a peacetime program requiring the full knowledge and assent of Congress.[18]

The proposed Atomic Energy Commission represented the Truman administration's whole plan for the military and peaceful development of atomic energy in the future. The Truman administration's acknowledgement of the crucial role the Congress was about to play in deciding the future of nuclear energy and the revolutionary implications of nuclear energy for war and peace are captured in a letter from President Truman to the House Committee on Military Affairs. President Truman's letter, which begins diplomatically by thanking Congress for enabling the United States to develop the atomic bomb during the wartime emergency, is carefully deferential to congressional power, sensitive to any misgivings by the Congress over the way the Manhattan Project was run. The letter asks the Congress to establish the AEC to preserve the scientific-industrial infrastructure and regulate the development of atomic weapons and energy, with all their great promise to transform the world. President Truman:

> The discovery of the means of releasing atomic energy began a new era in the history of civilization. The scientific and industrial knowledge on which this discovery rests does not relate merely to another weapon. It may some day prove to be more revolutionary in the development of human society than the invention of the wheel, the use of metals, or the steam and internal combustion engine.... Now that our enemies have surrendered, we should take immediate action to provide for the future use of this huge investment in brains and plant. I am informed that many of the people on whom depend the continued successful operation of the plants and the further development of atomic knowledge are getting ready to return to their normal pursuits.... Prompt action toward establishing a national policy will go a long way toward keeping a strong organization intact.[19]

Testifying on behalf of the proposed AEC for the Truman administration were its "biggest guns," Secretary of War Robert B. Patterson and leaders of the Manhattan Project, including General Leslie Groves, Vannevar Bush, James B. Conant, and Leo Szilard.[20] Szilard was a colleague of Albert Einstein and originally conceived the concept that became the atomic bomb. In the shadow of Hiroshima and Nagasaki, these Manhattan Project leaders and scientists were regarded by the press and public with awe.[21]

No doubt the Truman administration also hoped to awe the Congress in these hearings.

Secretary Patterson's testimony to the House Committee on Military Affairs noted that H.R. 4280 was drafted by a Presidential Commission that included General Groves and the other Manhattan Project leaders who were there to testify. Patterson's essential argument for the AEC was that the War Department should be divested of responsibility for atomic energy because it had peaceful applications that could lead to a new technological revolution and benefit all mankind. Patterson stressed that the proposed Atomic Energy Commission would be a creature of the Congress: "In all its activities the Commission would function under the basic principles laid down by Congress in this bill."[22]

General Groves too emphasized that the proposed Atomic Energy Commission would operate within limits defined by the Congress.[23]

Despite advocacy of H.R. 4280 and the AEC by the Manhattan Project's respected scientists, the House Committee on Military Affairs was enormously skeptical of the proposed Atomic Energy Commission. Prominent among the Committee's concerns was that the AEC might advance the Baruch Plan.

For example, Rep. R. Ewing Thomason emphasized that the AEC must not become a vehicle for giving away A-bomb secrets. Thomason doubted the wisdom of the Baruch Plan, the United Nations, and the principles of internationalism. U.S. atomic secrets should remain U.S. property, according to Thomason.[24] Rep. Dewey Short and Rep. John J. Sparkman wanted to be sure that the AEC legislation would not permit transfer of atomic technology to international control, that atomic technology would remain in possession of the United States.[25] Rep. Charles E. Clason raised more skepticism about the proposed AEC among Committee members when, on cross examination, he caught General Groves in a mistake. Contrary to the testimony of General Groves, the AEC legislation did not prohibit the service of foreign nationals in U.S. atomic programs, as foreign nationals had served in the Manhattan Project.[26] More damaging, Rep. J. Leroy Johnson voiced fears that the AEC would empower President Truman to trade atomic secrets at upcoming summits on the United Nations to build international support for the UN and advance the cause of "world peace." General Groves' reply appeared to confirm these congressional fears.[27]

Other concerns about the proposed AEC were raised by the Chairman of the Military Affairs Committee, Rep. Andrew J. May, who worried about the extent of the AEC's powers over civilians and whether it could compel scientists to serve, and so violate civil liberties.[28] Rep. Thomas E. Martin, Rep. Charles H. Elston, and Rep. John Edward Sheridan raised many objections to the proposed AEC. They voiced concerns that the AEC would have too much power to appropriate property and draft contracts outside the normal boundaries of law. Giving the AEC, and so the U.S. government, power over nuclear energy was concentrating too much power in the executive branch and the agencies of the federal government relative to the private sector, in the view of many in Congress. Indeed, in their view, since atomic energy represented the future, giving federal bureaucrats exclusive control over atomic energy would give the White House and its government minions too much power over the future development of the nation.[29]

Perhaps most damaging to the proposed legislation for the AEC, Rep. Clason objected that H.R. 4280 cut Congress out as an active participant in the development and oversight of nuclear energy. General Groves appeared to agree with this criticism:

CLASON: ...if the bill is passed...Congress is out of the picture except as regards appropriations?
GROVES: Yes.[30]

Rep Leslie C. Arends proposed an alternative bill, H.R. 4152, that would more clearly empower Congress to regulate nuclear matters.[31]

Instead of rubberstamping into existence the Truman administration's proposed AEC, the Congress moved immediately to establish its own oversight of nuclear weapons and energy. Senate Resolution 179 established the Special Committee on Atomic Energy. Chaired by Senator Brien McMahon, the Special Committee had a broad charter to gather data and investigate the scientific, industrial, economic and social significance of atomic energy and served as a basis for evaluating any future bills on its control:

> *Resolved.* That a special committee on atomic energy to be composed of eleven Members of the Senate appointed by the President pro tempore of the Senate, of whom one shall be designated as chairman by the President tempore, is authorized and directed to make a full, complete, and continuing study and investigation with respect to problems relating to the development, use, and control of atomic energy. All bills and resolutions introduced in the Senate, and all bills and resolutions from the House of Representatives proposing legislation relating to the development, use, and control of atomic energy shall be referred to the special committee.[32]

Four months after the Nagasaki bombing, the U.S. Senate's Special Committee on Atomic Energy convened its first hearings, in November and December 1945. These hearings were in-depth interviews with Manhattan Project scientists on how atomic bombs are built, their effects, and the costs and characteristics of the scientific-industrial infrastructure necessary to sustain the atomic program. General Groves provided crucial testimony at these hearings that emphasized that the Los Alamos atomic laboratory and other scientific-industrial facilities could perish and that if they were allowed to close, they could not be reconstituted. These hearings played an important role in persuading Congress to continue funding the U.S. atomic infrastructure inherited from the Manhattan Project.[33]

Yet despite general agreement between Congress and the Truman administration on the necessity of continuing the atomic labs and industries, the 1945 hearings of the Special Committee on Atomic Energy brought into sharper relief differences between the Congress and the Truman administration over internationalizing atomic energy. For example, at these hearings General Groves testified that, because of the invention of atomic weapons, "I think you have got, maybe, to change the world from feeling loyalty to nations."[34] Vannevar Bush testified that the United Nations Charter represented a "high point" among the achievements of mankind, and that UN international control and an international inspection regime was the best future for atomic energy.[35]

Chairman McMahon sharply challenged these views. Representing the overwhelmingly dominant opinion of the Special Committee on Atomic Energy, Chairman McMahon doubted Bush's assertions that potential enemies would stop pursuing atomic weapons, and surrender nationalism for internationalism, to avoid atomic war and reap the benefits of the "peaceful atom."[36]

Perhaps most remarkable about the 1945 hearings of the Special Committee on Atomic Energy was how quickly Congress advanced its own "learning curve" so that by December 1945, some of the most advanced thinking about the future of atomic weapons and their implications for warfare was happening in the Congress. For example, at the December 1945 hearings of the Special Committee, its members encouraged the Navy to explore atomic energy as a means of powering ships. The Committee received testimony from Dr. Ross Gunn, a Navy researcher who had been conducting rudimentary experiments on atomic powered ships since 1939.

Presciently, Senator Edwin C. Johnson of the Special Committee suggested to Vice Admiral W.H.P. Blandy, the Deputy Chief of Naval Operations for Special Weapons, that atomic power should be used to power submarines. Senator Johnson also suggested that the best way to protect U.S. cities from atomic attack might be with an atomic deterrent based at sea, an observation that prompted Rear Admiral William R. Purnell to suggest that submarine-launched ballistic missiles might be the best way to deliver atomic weapons.[37]

The Special Committee on Atomic Energy, as early as its December 1945 hearings, pushed hard to make these visionary possibilities for atomic weapons practical realities. At the December 1945 hearings, Chairman McMahon pressed the Navy to move quickly to incorporate atomic weapons into naval operations. Told by Admiral Blandy that the Navy planned to conduct an atomic test to study the effects of A-bombs on ships, Chairman McMahon urged the admiral not to wait for test results, but to start planning for atomic war at sea right away. McMahon also directed that a board of scientists be present at the Navy atomic test to ensure that the service was not accused of skewing test data to support their programs.[38]

The enthusiasm for atomic weapons in the U.S. Senate's Special Committee on Atomic Energy contrasted sharply with the views of J. Robert Oppenheimer, scientific leader of the Manhattan Project. Testifying before the Special Committee, Oppenheimer advocated against building a stockpile of atomic bombs: "I think everyone must accept, and I think everyone can be persuaded to accept, the undesirability of atomic armament." Oppenheimer:

> There is one thing that I should add, not as a technical witness, but as a citizen. Today all nations, all peoples, have an overriding community of interest in the prevention of atomic warfare. There would thus seem to be good reason to establish in the international control of atomic armament those patterns of confidence, collaboration, and good faith which in a wider application must form the basis of peace....There may not be a comparable opportunity again....the building of a stockpile of bombs, when we don't intend to use them...would give

us an absolutely illusory security. An atomic bomb which you do not use is of no use to you.[39]

Oppenheimer's vision, sounding like the original prototype for "ban the bomb" activism, contrasted sharply with the vision of Chairman McMahon and the other "atomic warriors" who dominated the Special Committee. For example, responding to Oppenheimer, Senator Eugene D. Milliken suggested that the best defense against A-bombs might not be disarmament, but launching a preemptive strike.[40]

Oppenheimer's personal views supporting nuclear disarmament, though not representative of the mainstream policy of the Truman administration, inflamed congressional suspicions and moved the Congress to be more jealous of its oversight prerogatives and more aggressive in asserting them over the atomic weapons and energy program.

In June 1946, the Special Committee on Atomic Energy introduced the "McMahon Bill," Senate Resolution 1717, "An Act for the Control of Atomic Energy." This rewrote the original bill for the Atomic Energy Commission in terms acceptable to the Special Committee and became the basis for establishment of the AEC. Whereas the earlier bill minimized the role of Congress, the new bill put Congress in charge of the AEC and clearly in the driver's seat of atomic energy development.[41]

From the congressional perspective, the most important part of S.R. 1717 was Section 14, which established the Joint Committee on Atomic Energy (JCAE). The JCAE succeeded the Special Committee on Atomic Energy and expanded its power to include oversight for the AEC. The JCAE was a new and unusual congressional committee in that it comprised members from both houses--nine Senators and nine House Representatives, a configuration that greatly increased the JCAE's power and influence compared to the original Special Committee.[42]

Other changes to the Atomic Energy Commission in S.R. 1717 included the Vandenberg Amendment, which expressly prohibited secret information on the design of atomic weapons from being shared with other nations.[43] Congress also amended the AEC so that it would not be "fiscally reckless" and included rigorous oversight provisions for accounting by the Comptroller General.[44] The free-wheeling days of the Manhattan Project were clearly over.

Also gone by June 1946 in S.R. 1717, less than one year after the Hiroshima and Nagasaki bombings, was any ambiguity about the legally dominant role of the Congress in deciding the future development of atomic weapons and energy, as General Groves learned the hard way. At a hearing on the bill, Chairman McMahon chastised General Groves for arguing that defense against atomic weapons is impossible, a key argument for international control and abolition.[45] The Senate rejected Groves' suggestion that S.R. 1717 should have language allowing the possibility that the United States does not want atomic weapons for all time, that abolition of atomic weapons is possible.[46] Finally, under pointed questioning by Senator Arthur H. Vandenberg, General Groves acknowledged that Congress should be in charge of atomic energy, that he would obey the Congress over the President on matters of atomic energy, and that he supported the congressional inclusion in the AEC bill of the Joint Committee on Atomic Energy, which had no representation from the executive branch.[47]

Congress, with the establishment of its version of the Atomic Energy Commission, saved and began the expansion of the atomic scientific-industrial infrastructure at Los Alamos, Argonne, Oak Ridge, Hanford and elsewhere. But of equal or greater significance for the future strategic posture was the role of Congress in forging the National Security Act of 1947.

The National Security Act of 1947 reorganized the U.S. national security establishment to meet the more demanding requirements of maintaining peace and fighting wars in the atomic age. "Reorganized" is perhaps too pedestrian a term for what was, in fact, a revolution in thinking about and preparing for future wars, which were the chief rationales for this Act.

Since the end of World War II, one of the chief preoccupations of the Congress was the reorganization of the national security establishment and the creation of new institutions to cope with a more demanding peacetime threat environment and with more demanding future wars. The experience of World War II had dramatically changed the threat perceptions of most Americans, whether they worked in the White House or the Congress, in factories or on farms. Gone were the days of comfortable pre-Pearl Harbor isolationism, when Americans believed overwhelmingly that the United States could avoid world wars by shunning entangling alliances with Europe. Gone were the days when the Atlantic and Pacific oceans were perceived as moats that would reliably protect America from future aggression, or at least give the United States time to mobilize to defend itself, as it had done during World War II.

Military existing and emerging technology--atomic weapons, bombers, missiles-- appeared to dictate a radical change from historical norms in the overall military posture of the United States. Given the geopolitics of 1945 and its emergence as the leader of the Free World, the United States could not afford to return to a state of military unpreparedness, of virtual disarmament, as after World War I and other wars. The United States could not afford another Pearl Harbor in the atomic age.

After World War II, the Congress worked for two years with the White House, the War Department, and the military services to forge a plan for new institutional arrangements that would permanently reconstruct the military posture of the United States to survive and prevail in wars of the future. The Senate and House military committees were the primary workshops where the concept for the new U.S. posture was negotiated and hammered into an organizational reality. The process consumed much of the time of the Congress between 1945 and 1947, and it was certainly one of the most formidable tasks ever taken on by the legislative branch. The paper trail alone, from a historian's perspective, literally speaks volumes about the scale of the impressive feat that produced a record of hearings and briefings and bill drafts that may be stacked yards high. The ambitious scope of this feat is also communicated by the name of early bill drafts--such as the 1946 draft bill Senate Resolution 2044 "Unification of the Armed Forces," which eventually became the National Security Act of 1947.[48]

The purpose of the National Security Act of 1947 was to create a new U.S. military and strategic posture that could maintain a high level of preparedness in peacetime sufficient to deter or defeat enemy aggression. The Act reorganized the military services and "unified" them under the Department of Defense, newly created by the Act, to manage a more efficient and more effective war machine and coordinate acquisition of military capabilities and formulation of plans. The Act also created other new institutions, external to the Defense Department that nonetheless would play important roles in the future U.S. military and strategic posture.[49]

Highlights of the National Security Act of 1947 include the following:

- The abolishment of the old War Department and its replacement with the new Department of Defense.

- The creation of the Joint Chiefs of Staff and a Chairman of the JCS.

- The re-establishment of the U.S. Army, Navy, Marines, and Air Force under the new Joint Chiefs of Staff structure.

- The creation of the National Security Council in the White House.

- The creation of the Central Intelligence Agency.[50]

Congressional hearings on the building of this new national security structure reiterated the theme that future wars were expected to be sudden, massively destructive from the onset, and decided by technology. According to numerous authorities giving testimony at the hearings, the future possibility of global war, especially atomic war, necessitated high peacetime military preparedness and peacetime coordination of all scientific, industrial, and military resources to ensure that U.S. military technology remained superior.

For example, at a 1946 hearing before the U.S. Senate Committee on Naval Affairs, Secretary of the Navy James Forrestal echoed the above views: "Strategic Decisions which direct the conduct of global war require deliberation and consultation....they are dependent upon tangibles and intangibles such as resources of manpower and material, political and industrial conditions, and maximum production of the sinews of war while still maintaining an acceptable minimum of production for the ordinary needs of life within the Nation."[51]

General Dwight Eisenhower, at a 1947 hearing on the "National Defense Establishment" before the Senate Armed Services Committee, testified that the proposed reorganization of the armed forces under a Secretary of Defense was needed for flexibility and greater military preparedness in this new age of scientific and technological war:

> Further, the broad powers of the Secretary will provide the one great element of a modern security structure which is markedly absent from our present organization. That is flexibility. In this day of scientific and technological war, it is of primary importance to balance the security forces against world conditions as they exist from year to year.[52]

General Lauris Norstad, Director of Plans and Operations for the War Department General Staff, in 1947 told the Senate, quoting the Strategic Bombing Survey, which reviewed the effects of strategic bombing on Japan and Germany, that a new "Department of Common Defense" was necessary to coordinate future war efforts and to protect U.S. cities from air and missile attack:

> Within a department of common defense which provides unity of command and is itself oriented toward air and new weapons, the survey believes that, in addition to the Army and the Navy, there should be an equal and coordinate position for a third establishment. To this establishment should be given primary responsibility

for passive and active defense against long-range attack on our cities, industries and other sustaining resources [and] for strategic attack whether by airplane or guided missile...[53]

General George C. Marshall's testimony to the Senate Armed Services Committee asked the Senate to impose the proposed reorganization of the national security establishment, in part to prevent the military services from wasteful and dangerous quarrels over the military posture and budgets.[54]

The CIA was instituted temporarily by Executive Order in January 1946. The CIA Director, General Hoyt S. Vandenberg, seeking permanent establishment of CIA by the Congress, testified to the Senate Armed Services Committee in 1947 that the Central Intelligence Agency was a necessity "in an era of atomic warfare" and that the nation could afford no more Pearl Harbors. Vandenberg: "In my opinion, a strong intelligence system is equally if not more essential in peace than in war....We must have this intelligence if we are to be forewarned against possible acts of aggression, and if we are to be armed against disaster in an era of atomic warfare."[55]

Likewise, Allen Dulles wrote to the Senate to justify permanent establishment of the CIA because future intelligence would be different and more scientific. Atomic energy and missiles were now more important than conventional military intelligence: "The prime objectives today are not solely strategic or military, important as these may be. They are scientific--in the field of atomic energy, guided missiles, supersonic aircraft, and the like."[56]

The congressional perspective was well captured by a Senate witness, Admiral Ernest King, who at a 1946 hearing declared that Congress now had an unprecedented role in organizing national defense. Congress mattered more than ever because wars were no longer fought by the armed forces alone, but rather by the whole industrial and scientific might of the

nation. Admiral King:

> Now that we are at the close of the war with the Axis Powers, ways and means are
> being sought to improve our national defense.... Congress has its full share....The
> term "national (common) defense" is used advisedly and in the sense that it
> includes in this country which has an important bearing on our national security.
> Wars are no longer fought solely by armed forces. The whole citizenry and the
> entire resources of a nation go to war, directly or indirectly. The war which has
> just closed demonstrates that fact clearly.[57]

Or as Senator Peter G. Gerry simply put it, "this atomic bomb changes everything."[58]

Congress by 1947 had laid the foundations, formed the "tectonic plates," upon which the

future U.S. strategic posture and the overall U.S. military posture would rise for decades to

come. The national nuclear laboratories and defense industrial infrastructure at Los Alamos,

Argonne, Oak Ridge, Hanford and elsewhere would design, test, and build nuclear weapons.

The Atomic Energy Commission and Joint Committee on Atomic Energy would oversee the

nuclear weapons infrastructure and the strategic thinking guiding weapons development. The

Department of Defense and the Joint Chiefs of Staff would provide a unified vision of the forces,

operations, and strategy that must be sustained and implemented by the military services in the

atomic age. The National Security Council, from its global perspective in the White House,

would provide presidential direction to the Department of Defense on overall national security

policy in the atomic age. The Central Intelligence Agency would assess strategic and technical

threats, so that U.S. forces could prepare to meet them and provide warning so that there would

be no more Pearl Harbors.

When Congress girded for the atomic age by passing the National Security Act of 1947,

Congress and the nation expected a protracted period of U.S. monopoly in atomic weapons. Two

years later, unforeseen by the CIA, the Soviet Union tested its first atomic bomb. Fears imagined for a more distant future were suddenly stark realities in the present, confronting a

United States that had just begun organizing for the Cold War.

Air Power

During the period of the U.S. monopoly in atomic weapons, between 1945-1948, the

United States possessed only 12 A-bombs and at first 5, but later 27, specialized B-29s capable

of delivering them.[59] These small numbers make the Baruch Plan or Oppenheimer's advocacy

of A-bomb abolition seem realistic visions of the future, as the United States and the world in

1948 were so near to "global zero" atomic weapons. But the Soviet Union ensured that these

alternative futures were not to be when it conducted its first A-bomb test, publicly disclosed by

President Truman on September 23, 1949.[60]

The sudden emergence of the Soviet Union as a rival atomic power surprised and

shocked most Americans and their political leaders. Although Congress was told in 1945 by

some witnesses, like General Groves, that the Soviets could get the A-bomb in 5 to 20 years,

most estimates leaned heavily toward a threat horizon of a decade or more.[61] Moreover, until

1949, there was hope among many that a Soviet atomic threat could be avoided through the

Baruch Plan and the United Nations, a hope that still persisted among some in the Department of

State until 1953.[62]

Spurred by the 1949 Soviet atomic test, the United States rapidly expanded its strategic

capabilities. By the end of 1956, the Strategic Air Command had 30 bomber wings with about

60 aircraft in each wing, for a total of about 1,900 strategic bombers, mostly B-47s (1,300) and

B-36s (400) capable of delivering thousands of atomic and nuclear bombs directly from the

United States to the Soviet heartland.[63]

Congress made possible this dramatic growth of U.S. strategic strength with its earlier decisions to sustain and expand the atomic weapons scientific-industrial infrastructure and create new national security institutions to meet the unprecedented military requirements of the Cold War.

Congress, in addition to providing the material and institutional sinews for Cold War defense and deterrence, also played a no less important role in the evolution of U.S. strategic thinking. The Air Force, Navy, and Army had different institutional interests that contributed to their different and often sharply conflicting perspectives on the nature of future war in the atomic age and on how best to be prepared. The clash of strategic ideas among the Air Force, the Navy, and the Army was waged mostly before Congress, often in connection with congressional hearings on authorization and appropriations for service programs and budgets. Service rivalries over their roles in the atomic era were so severe that in 1947, a dinner joke by Air Force General Frank Armstrong -- "That the air forces would be the dominant service of the future, that the Marine Corps would become part of the Army, and the Navy would play a substantially minor role,"-- prompted a congressional investigation to keep the peace.[64]

Congress and the military services understood that the atomic bomb represented a revolution in the U.S. strategic posture that created an opportunity for each of the services to achieve primacy over the others. Throughout this early Cold War period and afterwards, the Air Force, the Navy, and the Army offered competing theories of future war favorable to their own service, if not to achieve primacy, then at least to avoid irrelevance in the atomic era.

Congress was not merely a passive witness or a referee in the struggle among the services over strategic doctrine. Congress was the judge, had its own ideas, and, in the end, decided the victor. Until 1956, the victor was the strategic bomber and Air Power.

The 1948 debate before Congress over how the A-bomb would affect future war unfolded against a background of a growing crisis. Faced with possible communist takeovers in Greece and Turkey, President Truman in a surprise appearance before Congress, asked for and received funding to rescue these governments and announced on March 12, 1947 (the textbook date for the start of the Cold War) the Truman Doctrine, a policy to contain communist expansion. The Marshall Plan, to provide U.S. aid to reconstruct Europe in order to prevent communist revolutions or Soviet takeover, was approved overwhelmingly by the House and Senate and signed by President Truman on April 3, 1948. The Berlin crisis began with a Soviet blockade of the city on June 24, 1948, necessitating a massive U.S. airlift to support the troops and population in the allied sector of Berlin for a year, until the Soviet blockade ended in 1949.[65] The Berlin crisis prompted U.S. military planners, for the first time since Nagasaki, to propose to President Truman the atomic option.[66]

In 1948 hearings before the House Appropriations Committee, Secretary of the Air Force W. Stuart Symington made the case for Air Power in stark terms: slavery under communism could only be avoided if the United States had a strong Air Force. Symington: "The 'price of our security' as you might say must be balanced against the terrible consequences of defeat and slavery through failure to have developed adequate air power."[67] Secretary Symington cited the authority of the Congressional Aviation Policy Board that also gave primacy in the strategic posture to Air Power:

> To defend ourselves in the age of atomic bombs, or radioactive dust, of
> bacteriological contamination and guided missiles--to mention some of the new
> and terrible weapons--we must have air power that is supreme.[68]

Answering Secretary Symington, General Omar Bradley, Army Chief of Staff, in a 1948 hearing before the same Committee, observed that Congress would decide the future military posture: "I am convinced we can no longer defer a carefully planned development of the Army's capabilities.... Thus, the future military position of the United States and, concurrently, the degree of national security that our country may hope to enjoy in the future, rests with this Congress and with this committee."[69] General Bradley argued that atomic weapons made the Army more important than ever:

> You have already heard too many confusing and sometimes statements on the roles and combat functions of the several defense arms. Today I speak only of the Army. There is no doubt in my mind but that the role of our ground forces in defense of the country has been made more critical rather than lessened by atomic and air-age warfare. Without defense forces and without expeditionary forces to seize bases from which to launch air attack, even a sky full of air groups or carrier groups would be incapable of assuring victory.[70]

Truman's Secretary of Defense, Louis Johnson, convinced that part of Soviet strategy was to make the United States spend itself into bankruptcy on defense programs, imposed austerities by cancelling the Navy's 65,000 ton new generation aircraft carrier, the *United States*, in favor of funding the Air Force's B-36 strategic bomber.[71] The *United States* was the Navy's opening gambit to seize primacy from the Air Force in the strategic posture, as the "supercarrier" was designed to support both atomic and conventional air strikes from sea. Cancellation of the *United States* sparked what the press called "the Admiral's Revolt," wherein Navy spokesmen argued before Congress that the sole mission of the B-36, atomic warfare, was not strategically rational. Admiral Arthur W. Radford testified before the House Armed Services Committee that atomic war would be a war of annihilation that could serve no useful strategic purpose:

> One member of the defense team in one branch of the Government asserts that the best guarantee for America's security lies first in preventing war by the threat of atomic annihilation, and second in prosecuting such a war of annihilation if we have to fight....This theory of warfare is not generally concurred in, I believe, by military men. Aside from any moral or political considerations ...many reject the theory on the grounds that it will fail to bring victory.... [Moreover], future war will extend far beyond the province of the military. In planning to wage a war...we must look to the peace to follow...A war of annihilation might possibly

bring a Pyrrhic victory, but it would be politically and economically senseless...the results of two world wars have demonstrated the fact that victory in war is not an end in itself.[72]

The Congress gave primacy to Air Power. The Navy lost its carrier, and the Air Force got the B-36. But the debate continued.

In 1949 the Soviets tested the A-bomb. Congress overwhelmingly, by 83 to 13, approved the North Atlantic Treaty Organization, creating an alliance between the United States and Europe against Soviet aggression. Communism and Mao Zedong triumphed in China, with the retreat of General Chiang Kai-shek to Formosa, in December 1949. Communists in northern Korea invaded the south, launching the Korean War on June 25, 1950.[73]

The Korean War was also an important battleground within the Congress and between the services over the future strategic posture. The war was viewed as a real world test of the strategic theories that were in competition since the advent of atomic weapons and as a potentially decisive moment in the larger Cold War struggle. President Truman's highly controversial firing of the allied forces commander, General Douglas MacArthur, who promised to achieve victory in Korea if permitted to bomb China, sparked congressional hearings on the "Military Situation in the Far East."

Throughout 1951 the Congress held a major series of hearings in rare joint sessions of the Senate Armed Services Committee and Senate Foreign Relations Committee to examine the conduct of the Korean War and its larger strategic implications. Many in Congress were wary of the Truman administration's internationalism and suspected, as did Senator William F. Knowland, that President Truman was "soft on communism" and that this constrained a sufficiently aggressive war effort in Korea.[74]

Important features of the hearings were the testimony of General MacArthur and letters exchanged between General MacArthur and the Joint Chiefs of Staff, submitted to the Congress, advocating different theories about how the Korean War should be prosecuted. General MacArthur advocated widening the war, bombing Chinese forces in Manchuria and China itself, if necessary, bringing the Chinese Nationalists on Formosa into the war, applying whatever force necessary to achieve victory. In MacArthur's view, defeat in Asia would mean defeat in Europe, and in the wider Cold War. The Joint Chiefs of Staff disagreed, arguing that the Korean conflict could and should be contained, that the stakes were not sufficiently high to risk a new world war.[75]

Most in Congress supported General MacArthur's view, and his advocacy of decisive use of strategic Air Power. Indeed, the "Far East" hearings featured testimony by General Albert O. Wedemeyer, a military expert on the Far East appointed by Presidential Directive to report on Korea and China. Led on by Senator Leverett Saltonstall, General Wedemeyer promoted strategic Air Power and the Air Force as the decisive instruments in modern war. General Wedemeyer consigned the Army and Navy to lesser, supporting roles:

> SALTONSTALL: And just a final question. You believe as some of the other witnesses have testified, that we should concentrate a greater strength on the Air Force than we are doing now?
>
> WEDEMEYER: Senator Saltonstall, I would tell you gentlemen anything you can do to insure that our country has undisputed control of the air would bring us the greatest security that anything you can do. The Navy ought to be directed to protect our sea lanes, and it ought to work on the submarine menace.
>
> The Air Force ought to insure that we have tactical and strategic air controls, undisputed control. I just can't emphasize it too strongly. In my judgment that's it. The Army would just be required to seize, maintain, and control bases from which we can with increasing effectiveness operate these other two services.[76]

The Korean War could be won and a big land war in Asia avoided by decisive use of strategic bombing, according to General Wedemeyer.[77] General Emmet O'Donnell, chief of the 15th Air Force of the Strategic Air Command, testified that the United States should use the A-bomb in Korea.[78]

Senator Richard B. Russell, Chairman of the Armed Services Committee, representative of most congressional opinion at the "Far East" hearings, agreed with Generals Wedemeyer and O'Donnell.[79] However, in Senator McMahon's view, the Korean War could trigger World War III and proved the necessity of greater U.S. efforts for atomic war and civil defense preparedness. Addressing General MacArthur, Senator McMahon, Chairman of the Joint Committee on Atomic Energy, counseled better U.S. preparedness for atomic war before expanding the Korean conflict to China, and possibly the Soviet Union:

> General, it has been announced that the atomic weapons of today are of much greater potency than those that were exploded at Hiroshima. We can anticipate in the event of an atomic attack on this country, therefore, if General Vandenberg is correct when he says that 30 percent of the attacking forces of the enemy bombers might be shot down...meaning that 70 percent would get through, that we would have terrific casualties and horrible damage....
>
> General, it is not either your fault or my fault that the Civil Defense Administrator said the other day that too many people are still playing ostrich in the face of atomic warfare....
>
> General, we have not that program in existence at the present time...you have stated that if the enemy hits by surprise that that may well be the decisive blow.
>
> You have stated, in answer to my questions, that you cannot... tell us that Soviet Russia will not enter this war if we enlarge it to the mainland of China....
>
> Now, in view of all that, General, don't you think it would be the part of wisdom to get ourselves into that kind of situation where we can avoid this final decision blow before we take the chance of precipitating this struggle?[80]

The "Far East" hearings also included testimony from Truman's former Secretary of Defense, Louis Johnson, who credited Congress with saving Korea through the National Security

32

Act of 1947. Johnson apologized to the Congress and blamed himself and President Truman for underfunding the 1950 defense budget, against congressional criticism.[81]

The "Far East" hearings were not a total defeat for the Navy. Carriers proved so valuable in the Korean War that Congress supported the building of the *Forrestal* class of "supercarriers" that were comparable to the canceled *United States*.

The year after the 1951 "Far East" hearings, the United States tested the hydrogen bomb (H-bomb) in 1952. Dwight Eisenhower was elected President that same year, and went on to achieve the Korean Armistice on July 27, 1953, by means of atomic diplomacy. The Soviets tested the H-bomb in 1953. The thermonuclear H-bomb, much more powerful than the fission A-bomb, increased the threat to U.S. strategic bombers as the longer lethal radius of the H-bomb could destroy bombers even when airborne and flying away from their bases to escape. A series of RAND Corporation studies between 1953-1956, led by Albert J. Wohlstetter, concluded that U.S. strategic bombers were vulnerable to a surprise attack by Soviet bombers.[82] In February 1955 a Department of Defense panel of distinguished scientists, the Technological Capabilities Panel, chaired by MIT President James R. Killian, delivered their report *Meeting the Threat of Surprise Attack*. The Killian Report concurred with Wohlstetter's RAND reports about the vulnerability of U.S. strategic bombers, recommended greater dispersal, provisions to increase warning, and greatly accelerated scientific research and development on future weapons to keep ahead of the Soviets.[83]

The H-bomb, the RAND reports, and the Killian report led to another landmark series of hearings by the Senate Armed Services Committee titled "Study of Airpower" in 1956. The "Airpower" hearings were not just about Air Power, but were a continuation of the battle among the Air Force, the Navy, and the Army over their theories of future war and respective roles. As the title of the hearings indicated, Congress already favored the Air Force.

General Curtis LeMay, chief of the Strategic Air Command, best represented the Air Force view at the "Airpower" hearings. A future world war would be an atomic and nuclear exchange delivered by long-range strategic bombers between the homelands of the United States and the USSR. Surprise attack by the Soviets would be the most likely scenario, attempting an atomic Pearl Harbor against U.S. bomber bases and cities. There would be no time for mobilization; the war would be won or lost with existing Air Power. LeMay briefed the Senate Armed Service Committee on a Soviet surprise attack scenario previously shared only with the Joint Chiefs, the National Security Council, and the CIA. A National Intelligence Estimate cited at the "Airpower" hearing concluded that the Soviet bomber force would be strong enough for an atomic attack on the United States within that same year, 1956. Fifty Soviet atomic bombs delivered against the United States could destroy an estimated 40 percent of U.S. population and 60 percent of industry.[84]

General LeMay assured the Congress that the Strategic Air Command was always on high alert, ready for any war the Soviets might start, and would achieve victory. General LeMay: "Under any reasonable set of assumptions we believe we now have the capability of winning any war the Soviets might start. We are not capable of winning it without this country receiving very serious damage. Five years ago we could have won the war without the country receiving comparatively serious damage."[85]

Admiral Robert B. Carney testified at the "Airpower" hearings that the Navy was vital in an atomic war: "In the event of nonatomic struggles, our various international security arrangements would be absolutely meaningless if the jugular sea arteries were severed, and even in the event of atomic war, loss of the seas could be the deciding factor in the case that tough nations were willing and able to fight on after the initial exchange of crippling atomic blows."[86]

Admiral Arleigh Burke, Chief of Navy Operations, testified at the "Airpower" hearings that the Navy would be the chief defense of the Free World because Navy carriers alone might be the only force to survive a Soviet surprise attack. Carriers at sea would be hard to find and safe from attack. Atomic bombs were a bigger threat to the Army and Air Force, according to Admiral Burke. More importantly, future wars were more likely to be small wars and much less likely to be an atomic world war. Therefore, the Navy, because of its greater flexibility to prosecute atomic war and small conventional wars, was more valuable than the Air Force, which was focused on the worst case, but least likely, contingency--all-out atomic war. Admiral Burke:

> Only by use of the sea can we give continuing and massive support to our allies and our Armed Forces deployed overseas....The free world cannot stand together if the United States Navy should be unable to insure freedom of the seas....
>
> Our forces must be able to withstand surprise attack, and strike immediate, powerful, telling blows in return. Survival under nuclear attack requires a high degree of mobility and dispersion, both of which are basic characteristics of naval forces. If a general war should start with a surprise atomic attack, naval forces operating well dispersed at sea will play an important part in immediate retaliation. After the first blows on the principal stationary targets are struck by both sides, our mobile far-ranging Navy alone may remain sufficiently undamaged to carry forward a continuingly powerful attack....
>
> ...I believe that a general war is getting less and less likely, because we will not start a general war, surely. Russia will not start a general war unless her leaders are convinced that she can win it without too much cost....At the same time you can never count for sure on that. There may be an insane man who can persuade his people to follow him.[87]

General Maxwell Taylor, Chief of Staff of the Army, testified at the "Airpower" hearings that the Army would be the most important service in a future war. The very effectiveness of the Strategic Air Command ensured that there would be an atomic stalemate, so atomic war would be unlikely. Small conventional wars were likely for the future. Only the Army could invade and occupy enemy territory, historically the only way to bring a war to a successful conclusion.

General Taylor:

> As we look to the future, it seems to us that the threat to our security poses itself in two general forms: first, general nuclear war, or, second, the piecemeal erosion of the free world through actions short of general war.
>
> Now, as we see nuclear weapons becoming available to ourselves and to a possible adversary, we are impressed with the fact that we have either reached, or are likely to reach in the near future, a condition where each side can virtually destroy the other. In other words, we are approaching that era, which we often call a period of mutual deterrence....
>
> However, as we estimate the probable effects of mutual deterrence, it seems that great general war, as a deliberate act, becomes less likely, and that the second danger of piecemeal erosion becomes increasingly likely....
>
> I would mention just a few of the forces which, in my judgment, make this Army contribution to deterrence. I would mention in the first category our deployments overseas. Our forces are deployed along the Iron and Bamboo Curtains. They are a reminder that any aggression in this particular area will be countered at once by the might of the United States.[88]

The Congress was perhaps even more enthusiastic about Air Power than General LeMay. Senator Stuart Symington, Chairman of the Air Force Subcommittee of the Senate Armed Services Committee, and former Secretary of the Air Force under Truman, at the "Airpower" hearings urged General LeMay to "tell the truth" as to whether Eisenhower administration cuts to the Strategic Air Command budget had eroded the strategic posture.[89] Chairman Symington agreed with General LeMay that, after a Soviet surprise atomic attack, the United States could still achieve victory. Chairman Symington and Senator Henry M. Jackson challenged Navy arguments that carriers would likely survive an atomic surprise attack, as the Navy was counting on warning from troop movements:

> JACKSON: I have a hunch that if they are going to engage in an all-out atomic war they are not going to tip their hand by a 30-day movement of troops. To exploit the advantage of the atom I would think that they would make the most of surprise.

The reason I mention this is that our previous witnesses feel that is definitely the line of approach or attack that they would make. It makes a lot of common sense.

ADMIRAL COMBS: Yes, sir. I think it does.[90]

The Congress, led by Chairman Symington, advocated and succeeded in increasing the number of B-52 strategic bomber wings from 11 to 17 to strengthen the U.S. strategic posture against a Soviet surprise atomic attack.[91] Senator Jackson successfully advocated accelerated production of the new B-52 bomber to fill the new wings.[92]

Congress in 1956 was clearly focused on building a strategic posture centered on bombers and Air Power. 1957 would see the USSR demonstrate another revolutionary new military capability--the Intercontinental Ballistic Missile (ICBM). The ICBM, mated with the thermonuclear warhead, threatened to make strategic bombers obsolete. On the U.S. side, Congress was largely responsible for the development of this revolutionary new thermonuclear weapon that by 1956 was already threatening the Air Power of the United States.

The H-Bomb

Congress played a crucial role in the development of thermonuclear weapons, which were so much more powerful than atomic weapons that the H-bomb represented yet another great escalation in destructive capability with potentially revolutionary military implications comparable to the original invention of the A-bomb. Many influential leaders in the scientific community, like J. Robert Oppenheimer and Hans Bethe, and in the Truman administration's Atomic Energy Commission, opposed development of the H-bomb on moral, practical, and strategic grounds. Opponents argued that the H-bomb would escalate the arms race, be too costly, and thwart the Truman administration's effort to achieve international accord on control of atomic energy through the United Nations and the Baruch Plan.

Previously Top Secret, now declassified, records of congressional hearings before the Joint Committee on Atomic Energy reveal that the JCAE probably saved the H-bomb from being scuttled. Moreover, the records indicate that the JCAE overcame opposition by the AEC to establish a second nuclear weapons laboratory, at Lawrence Livermore, to accelerate H-bomb development.

A survey of the declassified congressional records indicates that the Joint Committee on Atomic Energy, wielding its congressional powers and under the aggressive leadership of its Chairman, Senator Brien McMahon, was at least as important as the Atomic Energy Commission or any other institution in shaping the U.S. strategic posture.

In a Top Secret, now declassified, hearing of the Joint Committee on Atomic Energy in 1950, Dr. Edward Teller sought help from the JCAE to save his H-bomb project. Teller's testimony complained of inadequate funding for his project from the Atomic Energy Commission. The JCAE promised Teller he would receive funding. Chairman McMahon: "Dr. Teller has believed that we should go with full speed on the hydrogen bomb, and is also exceedingly anxious that we get right into the project as soon as possible. I told him that we wanted to be as helpful along those lines as possible."[93] They discussed the Fuchs Case and the threat from other communist atomic spies and the possibility that espionage enabled the Soviet Union to develop the A-bomb more quickly than expected. Soviet spies might give them the lead on the H-bomb. Teller agreed. Moreover, Teller warned that the USSR might be ahead on the H-bomb because, after World War II, the Los Alamos nuclear weapons laboratory lost many scientists and technicians who went back to peacetime work, and weapons development slowed. Teller also noted that many U.S. scientists were opposed to the H-bomb on moral grounds. The JCAE asked Teller for guidance on how to persuade scientists to work on the H-bomb.[94]

A Top Secret, now declassified, hearing of the Joint Committee on Atomic Energy on January 9, 1950 is especially illustrative of the JCAE's crucial role in the development of the H-bomb. Chairman McMahon expressed outrage at the hearing that President Truman's General Advisory Committee, led by J. Robert Oppenheimer, recommended that the United States not develop the H-bomb.[95] Alarmed that the Truman administration might abandon the thermonuclear project, Senator Millard Tydings spoke for the entire JCAE with the opinion that "the Soviets will have a gun at our heart if they do it [develop the H-bomb] and we do not."[96] The JCAE added $300 million more to the budget for infrastructure to support the thermonuclear project.[97] Chairman McMahon, on behalf of the JCAE, sent a lengthy letter to President Truman rebutting Oppenheimer's GAC Report in meticulous detail, and demanding that the President notify the JCAE of any executive decision not to "press ahead" with the H-bomb. The opening paragraphs of Chairman McMahon's letter to President Truman read in part:

> The profundity of the atomic crisis which has now overtaken us cannot, in my judgment, be exaggerated. The specific decision that you must make regarding the super bomb is one of the greatest ever to confront an American president. This letter, reflecting ideas stimulated by a number of recent conferences which I attended at Washington, Los Alamos, Argonne, Hanford, and elsewhere, is written in sincere hopes of being helpful to you....

> Those who oppose an all-out "crash" effort on the super impress me as being so horrified at the path down which the world is traveling that they have lost contact with common sense and reality.[98]

A previously Top Secret hearing of the Joint Committee on Atomic Energy on February 10, 1950 noted approvingly that the White House on January 31 sent a letter to the Atomic Energy Commission directing the AEC to work on the H-bomb. President Truman wrote, "I hereby direct the Atomic Energy Commission to proceed to determine the technical feasibility of a thermonuclear weapon..."[99] Chairman McMahon chastised the witness, an AEC Commissioner, reminding him that the AEC was legally obligated to report everything it did to the JCAE. The Chairman made clear his expectation that work on the H-bomb should be pursued aggressively. A JCAE member, Senator Tydings, urged the AEC to give priority to the H-bomb over everything else, including work on the peaceful applications of atomic energy. Chairman McMahon strategized with other JCAE members about how to hide H-bomb funding from the Appropriations Committee.[100]

A Top Secret, now declassified, hearing of the Joint Committee on Atomic Energy on March 10, 1950, again highlights the JCAE's aggressive advocacy of atomic weapons. Chairman McMahon conferred with JCAE members on their plans to appropriate more money for expanding the atomic weapons infrastructure and attracting more scientists to work on nuclear weapons.[101] Chairman McMahon wrote a letter on behalf of the JCAE, submitted to the hearing record, querying the Department of Defense and the Joint Chiefs of Staff whether enough was being done to build atomic weapons. The JCAE noted that the Soviet A-bomb came as a surprise, and that U.S. was spending only one percent of its national budget on atomic weapons. The JCAE letter to the Secretary of Defense read in part:

> The Joint Committee on Atomic Energy have regularly considered individual programs in the Atomic Energy Commission budget, but can only judge the adequacy of the budget as a whole with your help and the help of the Joint Chiefs of Staff....
>
> I note that since the war we have devoted somewhat less than one-fortieth of our total military spending to atomic weapons, that is exclusive of methods of delivery and somewhat less than one percent of our total national budget to this purpose. Our current scale of effort is similar.
>
> Specifically, do you now regard and do the Joint Chiefs now regard such a scale of effort as adequate to the defense of the United States?[102]

At the March 10, 1950 hearing, Chairman McMahon and JCAE members discussed the use of legal means to force President Truman to spend more on atomic bombs and weapons development.[103]

A previously Top Secret hearing of the Joint Committee on Atomic Energy on March 28, 1950 further evidences the JCAE driving forward the H-bomb program. Chairman McMahon wrote a letter on behalf of the JCAE, submitted for the hearing record, to the Secretary of State urging the recruitment of British scientists to help accelerate U.S. development of the H-bomb:

> The Joint Committee on Atomic Energy is much troubled over the current difficulty in recruiting scientists and technical people for our hydrogen program. Testimony has been given to the Committee to the effect that the assistance of key British experts in the field of weapons is urgently needed.[104]

The JCAE also discussed how to secure Canadian cooperation and access to their NRX (National Research Experimental) Reactor at Chalk River, at the time the most powerful research reactor in the world, to advance the U.S. nuclear program without disclosing secrets to the Canadians. The hearing also illustrates JCAE's willingness to assert its authority over the Atomic Energy Commission. Senator Bourke B. Hickenlooper demanded that the witness, a representative of the Atomic Energy Commission, "toe the line" and comply with the Atomic Energy Act, which gave the JCAE oversight of the AEC. Chairman McMahon strongly concurred.[105]

In a Top Secret hearing, now declassified, of the Joint Committee on Atomic Energy on May 3, 1950, the JCAE members vigorously rebutted the arguments of their witness, Hans Bethe, one of the chief opponents of the H-bomb. After describing how the H-bomb is supposed to work, and the technical problems to be overcome, Bethe opined against building the H-bomb, saying it would be too costly. Bethe argued that A-bombs are more cost-effective, that more atomic weapons could destroy a greater area, at lesser cost, compared to the H-bomb. Chairman McMahon and Senator Henry Jackson disagreed, noting that the same argument could be used to ban A-bombs in favor of conventional bombs. Senator Jackson also noted that the U.S. would suffer a disastrous propaganda defeat and plummeting of morale if the Soviet Union were to get the H-bomb first.[106] Chairman McMahon also argued that the H-bomb was needed because hundreds of A-bombs would be required to destroy Russia. Chairman McMahon: "Of course...in Blackett's book he went on at great length to prove that it would take 400 A-bombs to do the same damage on Germany as was done in four years of conventional bombing. By that he extrapolated and figured out it would take God knows how much to do the job on Russia."[107]

A previously Top Secret hearing of the Joint Committee on Atomic Energy on September 28, 1951, features a JCAE Staff Report reviewing progress on H-bomb development. At the hearing, JCAE members advanced their plans to establish a second nuclear weapons laboratory to rival the Los Alamos laboratory in order to spur competition and accelerate development of new atomic and thermonuclear weapons. Chairman McMahon pressed for the development of an actual thermonuclear weapon as soon as possible, not just a test device, but a deliverable H-bomb.[108] Senator Jackson expressed the view that the H-bomb could be used in the ongoing Korean War:

> We have always talked about the hydrogen bomb in terms of strategic use, and I think, as I said the other day over here, the greatest mistake we have made is that we have allowed these tremendous weapons to be associated with the killing of women and children.
>
> I am not criticizing anybody; we are all to blame. If the bomb some way or another could have been used tactically in the beginning, it could be used in Korea today.[109]

A Top Secret hearing, now declassified, of the Joint Committee on Atomic Energy on February 21, 1952, featured a JCAE Staff Report judging that Russia was probably ahead in developing and weaponizing the H-bomb. The JCAE hearing also reviewed a letter from the Atomic Energy Commission arguing against JCAE's plan to build a second nuclear weapons lab to spur competition on atomic and nuclear weapons development. The existing nuclear weapons lab at Los Alamos was sufficient for national security, according to the AEC. JCAE's decision to overrule the AEC resulted in the establishment of a second lab, known today as the Lawrence Livermore National Laboratory.[110]

Nine months later, on November 1, 1952, "Operation Mike" detonated the first U.S. thermonuclear device. "Mike" produced a yield of 10.4 megatons, over 1,000 times more powerful than the Hiroshima A-bomb, ushering in the next revolution in military technology sought by Dr. Teller, Chairman McMahon, and members of the JCAE.[111] The H-bomb even changed the language of strategic discourse, eventually replacing "atomic" with the word "nuclear" for weapons, energy, and research. Thus, spearheaded by the Joint Committee on Atomic Energy, the Congress overcame political and institutional opposition, and technical problems, to the development of the H-bomb.

Nine months after "Mike," the Soviet Union detonated their first H-bomb. Unlike the U.S. "Mike," which was a thermonuclear experimental device, not a weapon, the Soviets tested a deliverable nuclear weapon.[112] An H-bomb deliverable by an intercontinental missile, if it could be done, would constitute another great revolution in military affairs.

The ICBM

On October 4, 1957, one year after the "Airpower" hearings that ratified and advanced a U.S. monadic strategic posture dominated by the bomber, the USSR launched and orbited in quick succession two "Sputnik" satellites, one weighing over a half-ton. This was widely interpreted in the United States as proving that the Soviets would soon have, or already had, Intercontinental Ballistic Missiles (ICBMs) capable of delivering nuclear warheads against the United States, while the United States had nothing comparable. Sputnik constituted perhaps the greatest political, technological, and military challenge of the 1950s for the United States.

Congress rose to the ICBM challenge, becoming arguably the most important institutional force driving forward the neglected U.S. ICBM program. Congress overcame Air Force reluctance to develop the new ICBM technology, which challenged the strategic primacy of the bomber. Congress also overcame Eisenhower administration reluctant to admit there was a crisis in the balance of power caused by the Soviet ICBM. The administration was loath to engage in a costly ICBM race with the USSR.

The H-bomb, with its much greater power and lethal radius when compared to the A-bomb, could compensate for the inaccuracy of the ballistic missiles of the day, made it possible for the Soviets to target reliably U.S. cities and Strategic Air Command bases in the United States using ICBMs. The great speed of ICBMs, theoretically capable of delivering a warhead from the other side of the planet to the United States in 30 minutes, posed an unprecedented challenge to U.S. strategic bombers, whose alert rates and strike plans were designed to thwart a surprise attack by relatively slow flying Soviet bombers, which, once launched, provided several hours of strategic warning. In 1955, the Killian Report warned that future invention of the ICBM would pose a serious challenge to the U.S. strategic posture.[113] One month after Sputnik, in November 1957, a Department of Defense panel of respected scientists delivered the classified Gaither Report to President Eisenhower's National Security Council, warning that the Soviet ICBM did indeed constitute an alarming threat of surprise attack.[114] Vannevar Bush, one of the most respected defense scientists in America, testified to Congress that Sputnik meant the USSR had achieved a strategic advantage: "So this is far more than merely a problem of an advance in weapons. This country now faces definitely a situation where it must prevent at all costs being in the position where it can be overcome without the possibility of answering."[115]

Although Congress responded rapidly to the ICBM challenge, Congress was also partly to blame for the United States losing the first round of the missile race to the USSR. Congress shared the Air Force's fascination with bombers, which during World War II and afterwards, were perceived as the "ultimate weapon." After all, the strategic bombing campaigns had laid waste to Germany and Japan, won the war in the Pacific with the A-bomb, constituted the most technologically sophisticated operations of World War II, boosted morale, and captured the popular imagination, regardless of the less enthusiastic technical evaluation of the *Strategic Bombing Survey*.[116] Many Congressman had served in bomber wings or believed their lives were spared by the atomic bombings of Japan. Moreover, after World War II, bombers appeared to be on the cutting edge of military technology. Breathtaking advances were made with the introduction of the B-36, which could travel intercontinental distances without refueling, and the jet-powered B-47, which made propellers an artifact of the past. The network of scientific labs, industries, and military bases that supported bomber development, production, and operations was probably among the greatest technological achievements in human history.

In contrast, before Sputnik, the ICBM was not taken seriously as a clear and present danger by the Air Force or the Congress, whose members viewed the ICBM as a potential threat technologically distant from the perspective of 1945, and even1957, prior to Sputnik. In December 1945, Vannevar Bush, one of the Manhattan Project scientific miracle workers, and then head of the Office of Scientific Research and Development, assured Congress that the ICBM was impossible:

> We have plenty enough to think about...so that we don't need to step out into some of these borderlines, which seem to me more or less fantastic. Let me say this: There has been a great deal said about a 3,000 mile high-angle rocket.
>
> In my opinion such a thing is impossible and will be impossible for many years. The people that have been writing these things that annoy me have been talking

about a 3,000 mile high-angle rocket shot from one continent to another carrying an atomic bomb, and so directed as to be a precise weapon which would land on a certain target such as this city… wish the American public would leave that out of their thinking.[117]

Between 1945 and 1958 the U.S. Air Force gave low priority to the ICBM program both because the Air Force believed bombers deserved highest priority and because the Air Force was not motivated to develop a technological rival to the bomber. The Army and Navy more aggressively pursued long-range missiles as a way of better fulfilling their military missions, and in the hope of breaking the Air Force monopoly on strategic Air Power; and possibly replacing the Air Force as the primary service in the U.S. strategic posture. But the Air Force worked skillfully with Congress to interfere with and takeover Army and Navy missile programs, which the Air Force then underfunded, keeping ICBM development on a slow track.[118]

Congressional hearings prove that the Congress was aware of the low priority being given to ICBM development. For example, in a 1948 hearing before Congress, the Air Force asked for and received permission to invest less money in ICBM development, which was described as a merely "experimental" program and occupied only one paragraph in a voluminous Air Force budget dedicated to bombers.[119] Moreover, some of the most respected and influential members of Congress, like Senator Symington and Senator Jackson, criticized in hearings the slow rate of ICBM development and warned that if the USSR developed ICBMs first, the United States could be subject to nuclear blackmail.[120] But there is no evidence that these Senators, who usually got what they wanted, acted on their opinions.

Immediately after Sputnik, in November 1957 and into 1958, the Congress launched a series of landmark hearings, "Inquiry Into Satellite And Missile Programs," which was a turning point for the Air Force ICBM program and the future U.S. strategic posture.[121]

The "Satellite and Missile" hearings were also a national phenomenon, heavily covered by the press for an American people who were shocked by Sputnik and looked to Washington for answers. Serious questions were raised in Congress and the nation whether the Free World could compete with the totalitarian Soviet Union that could focus all its national powers on a scientific-technological arms race. The Killian and Gaither Reports concluded that this was exactly the nature of the challenge, and that the ICBM did constitute a real threat, a technological Pearl Harbor. Senator Lyndon Baines Johnson captured well the view of Congress and the American public in his statement opening the 1957-1958 "Satellite and Missile" hearings":

> We are here today to inquire into the facts on the state of the nation's security. Our country is disturbed over the tremendous military and scientific achievement of Russia. Our people have believed that in the field of scientific weapons and in technology and science, we were well ahead of Russia.
>
> With the launching of Sputniks I and II, and with the information at hand of Russia's strength, our supremacy and even our equality has been challenged. We must meet this challenge quickly... We hope that when the testimony is finished, we will have a clear definition of the present threat to our security, perhaps the greatest that our country has ever known....
>
> The facts that I have learned so far give me no cause for comfort. I do not feel that they must be withheld from the public... It is not necessary to hold these hearings to determine that we have lost an important battle in technology. That has been demonstrated by the satellites that are whistling above our heads....In my opinion, we do not have as much time as we had after Pearl Harbor. [122]

The Army and Navy during the "Satellite and Missile" hearings made their bids to replace the Air Force as the primary service in the strategic posture. General Maxwell Taylor argued that the Army had an interest in rockets since the War of 1812 and that ICBMs were a natural extension of the Army mission, like long-range artillery. The Secretary of the Navy, Thomas S. Gates, urged that the advent of the Soviet ICBM meant that the United States should send its primary nuclear deterrent to sea by accelerating development of the Polaris submarine-launched ballistic missile. [123]

Even after Sputnik, the Air Force resisted calls for a crash program on ICBM development and defended strategic bombers as the weapons of the future. At the "Satellite and Missile" hearings General Curtis LeMay, chief of the Strategic Air Command, counseled Congress not to panic over Sputnik: "I would like to make one statement...in this atmosphere of sputniks and intercontinental missiles, when accusations and denials seem to be flying around the atmosphere of today, and that is I don't think any of us should be panicked by the fact that, apparently, our potential enemy is ahead of us in an armament race, or at least a portion of it."[124] LeMay continued to champion bombers over ICBMs, arguing that he could cope with an ICBM threat by dispersing and alerting the bomber force. The Secretary of the Air Force, James H. Douglas, assured the Congress that the Air Force was "open minded" about ICBMs and counseled an "evolutionary process" that sounded like a "go slow" approach that would ultimately favor bombers over ICBMs.[125]

Members of Congress had given strategic primacy to the Air Force, and lionized its leaders, like General LeMay, with whom they now had to fight over the future of the U.S. ICBM. Senator Johnson clashed with General LeMay, who wrongly tried to blame Congress for underfunding strategic bomber dispersal and alert programs, so that bombers could better survive an ICBM attack. But Senator Johnson prevailed:

> SEN. JOHNSON: Then is it not a little unfair to say Congress is to blame? If Congress had been asked to do this by the executive, and if we had considered it and refused to do so then we would be entitled to be blamed.
>
> ....You can appropriate funds to the executive but you cannot make him spend it. The two times we have appropriated additional money in substantial amounts to the Air Force, both times the executive refused to spend it; is that correct?
>
> GEN. LEMAY: I quite agree with you sir.[126]

Senator Weisl spoke for virtually everyone in Congress when he chastised Air Force Secretary Douglas for losing the ICBM race and trying to dodge responsibility:

SEN. WEISL: Mr. Secretary, the fact remains that the Russians have an engine with a thrust sufficient to project a thousand pound satellite in orbit, is that not so?

SEC. DOUGLAS: Yes, sir.

SEN. WEISL: We have it now?

SEC. DOUGLAS: Yes, sir.

SEN. WEISL: Where is it?

SEC. DOUGLAS: In all three programs.

SEN. WEISL: I am not talking about programs. It has been testified that we have no engine with a thrust sufficient enough to cast a thousand pound satellite in orbit with a guidance that will keep it in orbit.[127]

The Eisenhower administration was reluctant to acknowledge that the USSR's newly developing ICBM potential threatened the U.S. strategic posture. When the classified Gaither Report was delivered to the National Security Council in 1957, the frugal President Eisenhower privately was not pleased, since it called for copious spending on scientific and military research and development, though he made public comments consistent with its recommendations.[128] At the 1958 "Satellite and Missile" hearings Secretary of Defense Neil H. McElroy would not admit that the Eisenhower administration was behind the Soviets in ICBM development:

SEC. MCELROY: It is not clear to me that we are behind the Russians in overall missile development....

SEN. WEISL: Let me try to be more specific, Mr. Secretary. Are we ahead or behind the Russians in the development of the intercontinental ballistic missile?

SEC. MCELROY: I don't believe we have positive knowledge as to whether we are behind, and I'm quite sure we don't have positive knowledge as to whether we are ahead....

SEN. WEISL: Have you any basis for believing we are ahead in that field?

SEC. MCELROY: I have no basis for believing we are ahead.

SEN. WEISL: Have you any basis whatever for believing that we are behind in that field?

SEC. MCELROY: On a relative time basis, I do not have any such information....

SEN. WEISL: What other things do we have to know besides the fact that they have a rocket engine that can catapult a half-ton satellite into orbit?[129]

Senator Symington, himself a former Secretary of the Air Force, belittled Defense Secretary McElroy's claim that the USSR was not ahead in ICBMs: "You make that statement, Mr. Secretary, despite the now known greater Soviet accomplishments in the ICBM, the IRBM, the testimony of Dr. Teller, General Doolittle, their accomplishments, in thrust and propulsion as evidenced by the satellite, their production of jet aircraft, and their launching of the earth circling satellites, is that correct?"[130]

Lashed by criticism from Congress and the nation, the Eisenhower administration publicly accelerated the ICBM program at the "Satellite and Missile" hearings, but was spurred by Congress to do more. At the hearings, Defense Secretary McElroy announced that the U.S. Army's Jupiter and Thor medium-range missiles would be deployed at Air Force bases overseas. But Senator Weisl noted that the Jupiter had failed a flight-test "just yesterday." He also criticized as illogical a U.S. missile program that relied on the Army to build missiles for the Air Force.

SEN. WEISL: In other words the Army will have no control over the operation of the Jupiter when it becomes operational, and will not have any use for it in the performance of its roles or missions?

SEC. MCELROY: The Air Force will handle the operation of the Jupiter as well as the Thor.

SEN. WEISL: Do you believe, Mr. Secretary, that it is a wise use of brainpower and manpower to have the Army develop a missile that it will have no use for in the performance of its duty in case of war?[131]

Defense Secretary McElroy announced at the "Satellite and Missile" hearings that money for research and development proposed by Congress in the defense budget, but cut by the Eisenhower administration would be restored. Senator Harry Flood Byrd responded that Congress did not lose the ICBM race, but rather it was the Eisenhower administration, because of its defense cuts, that lost it.[132]

Finally, at the "Satellite and Missile Hearings," Secretary McElroy notified Congress that he would be asking the Congress to support increased funding for ICBMs and IRBMs.[133]

The "missile gap" would remain an important issue two years later in the 1960 election and help return Democrats to the White House with the election of John F. Kennedy. In fact, the Soviet Union was not deploying large numbers of ICBMs immediately after Sputnik, but had paused their program to develop a better missile. However, a real missile and bomber gap heavily favoring the USSR existed in medium-range missiles and bombers capable of targeting U.S. military bases and allies in Europe and Asia. Consequently, the greatly accelerated U.S. ICBM program carried the United States to a preponderant advantage over the USSR in ICBMs during the 1960s. This "missile gap" favorable to the United States contributed to the October 1962 Cuban missile crisis. It also greatly accelerated the Soviet ICBM program to close the "missile gap" with the United States and, in the 1970s, surpass the United States in ICBMs.

From the perspective of Congress and the nation in 1958, as reflected in the "Satellite and Missile" hearings, the United States faced a clear and present danger from the Soviet unilateral advantage in ICBM technology, which as yet had no equivalent in the U.S. strategic posture. Moreover, Sputnik appeared to prove that the United States was in an unprecedented and ever accelerating arms race, where today's "ultimate weapon" would be rendered obsolete tomorrow by yet a new generation of superweapons. Sober-minded people in 1958 did not think it unreasonable, looking back on the pace of technological development since 1945, to imagine that the decade of the 1960s might see orbital aerospace bombers and military bases on the moon.

Before Sputnik, the Eisenhower administration and Congress had started preparing for a technologically daunting future, while trying to protect the nation from bankruptcy in the process, by a strategic posture geared to the futuristic atomic age called the "New Look."

The New Look

President Eisenhower's "New Look" for the strategic posture, adopted in 1953, called for relying on atomic and nuclear firepower at the tactical and strategic levels and the development of smaller, lower-yield "miniaturized" atomic weapons for use by the Army on the battlefield and by the Navy in fighting at sea. New Look operational war plans incorporated the use of atomic and nuclear weapons as needed, under some circumstances as weapons of first choice, just like any other weapon. The New Look, it was hoped, would enable the United States to defend the Free World without bankrupting itself trying to build costly conventional forces and sustain mass armies and effectively compete with the armed forces of the USSR and Communist China. Moscow and Beijing fielded mass standing armies and enjoyed huge advantages in manpower, conventional forces, and geographic proximity to U.S. allies in Europe and Asia. The New Look would enable Washington to save money by relying on smaller force structures for the Army and Navy while increasing their military effectiveness and deterrent value through nuclear arms.

Congress since 1945 was thinking along similar lines and helped develop the technical and intellectual foundations that made the New Look possible.

President Eisenhower's New Look was not just Eisenhower's idea, and it was not really new. The World War II plans and operations leading to the atomic bombings of Hiroshima and Nagasaki were based on the same basic logic as the New Look--the exploitation of the destructive power of atomic weapons would save lives and resources and avoid a costly invasion of Japan. Since 1945 Congress, the military services, and the Truman and Eisenhower administrations all wanted to leverage the power of the atom to increase military effectiveness and buy U.S. national security on the cheap.

As the number of atomic weapons increased, and as the weapon design and delivery systems improved, the potential for their use in military operations also rose. Early war plans, like PINCHER in 1946 and FLEETWOOD, the latter developed after the 1948 Berlin crisis, focused on targeting Soviet cities because of the small number of U.S. atomic weapons then available.[134] But even these plans envisioned attacks on cities for the same military purposes pursued during World War II against Germany, to destroy Soviet war supporting industries, military transportation hubs, ammunition and fuel depots, and inflict massive civilian casualties to undermine morale. 1n 1949, Secretary of Defense James V. Forrestal convened the Harmon Committee to review U.S. atomic war plans. Critical of FLEETWOOD, the Harmon Committee concluded that FLEETWOOD would not necessarily defeat a Soviet invasion of Western Europe.[135] DROPSHOT, a requirements study conducted in 1949 in response to the findings of the Harmon Committee, indicated that the United States needed many more atomic weapons to destroy enough targets to defeat a Soviet invasion. The DROPSHOT study attacked some 700 targets, requiring 300 A-bombs and 20,000 tons of conventional bombs, to destroy the whole target set, which included cities, but mostly military targets, such as troop concentrations, naval targets, communications nodes, military supply lines, and depots.[136]

The New Look of 1953 was the product of a number of continuities that shaped all U.S. nuclear war plans and the strategic posture up that that point. First, nuclear strategy of the early Cold War continued the classical military tradition that based strategy and tactics on the best weapons available to achieve victory. Victory in nuclear war was not only considered possible, but it was the objective. Second, American strategic culture looked to solve military problems with technology first, a trait that helped drive the development of more imaginative uses for nuclear weapons. Third, economics and the desire to avoid a depletion of the treasury caused by maintaining large standing armies and navies against the Soviets drove the United States toward greater reliance on nuclear firepower. Finally, Air Force, Navy, and Army rivalry contributed significantly to wider roles for nuclear weapons.

Before the New Look of 1953, the military doctrines of the services and the Joint Chiefs of Staff sounded very much like the New Look. In 1948 the then-Top Secret Air Force manual *Doctrine of Atomic Air Warfare* stated: "Progression from the spear through the bow, musket, rifle and artillery to weapons of World War II was simply a matter of ever-increasing firepower....The atomic bomb does not appear to have deviated from this evolutionary trend."[137] In 1951, the Acting Chief of Navy Operations, L.D. McCormick wrote: "It is in our interest to convince the world at large that the use of atomic weapons is no less humane than the employment of an equivalent weight of so-called conventional weapons."[138] In December 1951, two years before the New Look, the Joint Chiefs of Staff stated: "It is United States policy on atomic warfare that, in the event of hostilities, the Department of Defense must be ready to utilize promptly and effectively all appropriate means available, including atomic weapons, in the interests of national security and therefore must plan accordingly."[139]

The New Look, while leveraging existing ideas and plans, was new in some important respects, mostly in its origins. NSC-68, a National Security Council study drafted in April 1950 just prior to the outbreak of the Korean War in June; and adopted just months after in September 1950, appeared prescient in warning that the communist bloc was becoming increasingly aggressive and determined to challenge the Free World globally. NSC-68 recommended the United States greatly increase its military preparedness to meet this challenge.[140] The experience of the Korean War, nearly a defeat; and costly, was an object lesson in what happens when the United States fights its adversaries on their terms. General MacArthur and most of the Congress had famously criticized the Truman administration for failing to bomb China and use the full weight of American power to achieve victory. President Eisenhower's successful termination of the Korean War, the armistice achieved by the threat to use tactical nuclear weapons, was an object lesson in what happens when the United States threatens to fight on its own terms; and can credibly play its nuclear "ace."[141] Finally, a growing scientific-industrial nuclear weapons infrastructure; that could produce greater numbers of nuclear weapons, and more technologically sophisticated nuclear weapons and delivery systems, for an ever wider range of purposes, made the New Look technically more feasible and credible.

The New Look was inaugurated on October 30, 1953, by NSC-162/2, and directed development of the following requirements for the United States:

1. a strong military posture, with emphasis on the capability for inflicting massive retaliatory damage by offensive striking power;

2. U.S. and Allied forces in readiness to move rapidly initially to counter aggression by Soviet bloc forces and to hold vital areas and lines of communication; and

3. a mobilization base, and its protection against crippling damage, adequate to ensure victory in the event of general war.

In the event of hostilities the United States will consider nuclear weapons be as available for use as other munitions.[142]

Histories often confuse the New Look with "Massive Retaliation," a phrase lifted by members of the press from a speech given by Secretary of State John Foster Dulles on January 12, 1954, to the Council on Foreign Relations, to explain the New Look. The press should have quoted this line from Dulles' speech: "...the Department of Defense and the Joint Chiefs of Staff can shape our military establishment to fit what is *our* policy, instead of having to try to be ready to meet the enemy's many choices. That permits a *selection* of military means instead of a multiplication of means."[143] Flexibility and deterrence and military effectiveness are all implied by these words, which more accurately convey what the New Look was really all about than does the phrase "Massive Retaliation."

The New Look was the culmination of ideas and capabilities that owed their existence in no small measure to the Congress. Congressional thinking since 1945 about atomic and nuclear weapons as military and strategic instruments anticipated the New Look. Congress helped solidify the strategic thinking of the Air Force, Army and Navy; as they sought to justify programs and budgetary primacy before Congress, in the process developing ideas and doctrines that anticipated the New Look, as shown earlier by military writings and statements.

Some examples of congressional thinking that anticipated the New Look, and congressional actions that made possible the New Look, follow.

As early as 1945, Senator Brien McMahon, Chairman of the Senate Committee on Atomic Energy, required the Navy to incorporate atomic weapons in Navy planning for future operations. Chairman McMahon supported Navy atomic tests to assess the effects of the A-bomb on fleets and ships and for planning atomic operations at sea.[144]

In 1945, eight years before the New Look, Senator Johnson of the Senate Committee on Atomic Energy was also already a proponent of Navy preparedness for tactical atomic war at sea. At a Top Secret (now declassified) hearing, Senator Johnson told Navy officials that he could not imagine a future world war where the A-bomb would not be used: "I cannot picture a world war in which they will not be used because of their vital effectiveness."[145] Moreover, Senator Johnson warned the Navy that, from the perspective of the Senate Committee on Atomic Energy, if the Navy did not prepare itself for atomic warfare, the Navy would become obsolete.[146]

In 1948, five years before the New Look, Senator Albert J. Engel and General Omar Bradley, Army Chief of Staff, already understood the tactical use of atomic weapons to support Army operations. Senator Engel, in a 1948 hearing, lectured General Bradley on the importance of troop dispersal and coordination on the future atomic battlefield, appearing to anticipate the basic tactics of what would later be called the Pentomic Division under the New Look. The Pentomic Division reorganized Army divisions and changed their operating tactics to avoid concentration of forces on the atomic battlefield, relying on the concentration and coordination of firepower, instead of massed troop and armor formations that would be easy atomic targets, a concept clearly anticipated both by Senator Engel and by General Bradley a half decade before the New Look:

> SEN. ENGEL: I do feel that as the destruction of the atomic bomb compels the dispersion of naval craft upon the high seas, so the same type of atomic warfare would require the dispersal of your troops.
>
> While you are not apportioning what I call the Army and its various service functions, you will, I think, be compelled to follow a wider dispersal of the mass concentration of men, and the concentration of men will become more dangerous in the atomic age.....

GEN BRADLEY: Yes sir. We realize that you have to disperse, not only in a concentration like a camp, but in actual battle. You are going to have to disperse, when the other fellow gets the atomic bomb.[147]

In 1950, three years before the New Look, the Joint Committee on Atomic Energy directed preparation of a Staff Paper on improving the readiness of the military services to employ atomic weapons. At a Top Secret, now declassified, hearing of the JCAE, Chairman McMahon favorably reviewed the Staff Paper recommendation that the military services be given custody of atomic weapons, except for their physics component, to improve service readiness for surprise attack and responsiveness to tactical situations.[148] The JCAE Staff Paper also noted, "Tactical uses: Staff conversations with the Defense Department indicate that the tactical use of atomic weapons is assuming increased importance and that the Navy may be expected to play a greater and greater role with respect to both the tactical and strategic use of such weapons."[149]

In 1950, the Joint Committee on Atomic Energy by letter recommended that the Secretary of Defense and the Joint Chiefs of Staff consider making greater use of atomic firepower in their plans and investing more in production of atomic weapons. In the same year, in a Top Secret (now declassified) hearing of the Joint Committee on Atomic Energy, Chairman McMahon advocated the advantages of the tactical use of atomic weapons.[150]

In 1951, Senator Jackson, at a previously Top Secret (now declassified) hearing of the Joint Committee on Atomic Energy, regretted the atomic bombings of Hiroshima and Nagasaki, because of the subsequent identification of A-bombs as weapons of mass destruction for killing women and children. In Senator Jackson's view, if the first A-bombs had been used tactically, against Japanese military targets, it would have set a better precedent for future use of nuclear weapons. The Senator opined that the H-bomb, then under development, could be usefully employed in the then ongoing Korean War.[151]

After the New Look, the Congress enthusiastically supported programs and policies for nuclearization of the Army and Navy--programs and policies long advocated by the Joint Committee on Atomic Energy. Congressional hearings and appropriations evidence the strong support by Congress for the nuclearization of the Army, for example, by development of the Pentomic Division. Congressional hearing and appropriation records indicate equally strong support by Congress for the nuclearization of the Navy through the integration of nuclear propulsion technologies on sea-going platforms and the provision of tactical nuclear weapons for operations at sea.[152]

By the end of the Eisenhower administration in 1960, President Eisenhower and the Congress had forged a strategic posture that prepared the United States for a nuclear World War III, and theoretically prepared the country for lesser tactical nuclear contingencies, such as another Korean War. The Strategic Air Command was on alert and ever ready to respond to a surprise nuclear attack from the USSR with massive strikes against the Soviet homeland. Congress authorized development and deployment of hundreds of ICBMs, including Atlas, Titan I, Titan II, and Minuteman I. The first ICBMs, 12 Atlas missiles, became operational by 1960. The first Single Integrated Operational Plan (SIOP), a master plan for global nuclear war to coordinate bomber and missile strikes, was drafted before President Eisenhower left office. The U.S. Army was prepared for theater and tactical nuclear warfare on the battlefields of Europe and Asia, to include use of the low-yield Davy Crockett, a nuclear bazooka that could be fired off the back of a jeep. The U.S. Navy was arming for strategic and tactical nuclear war at sea with submarines, carriers and ships, with weapons ranging from the Polaris strategic missile to the

Lulu anti-submarine atomic depth bomb. Nike air defense missiles, many armed with nuclear warheads, protected major U.S. cities and military bases.

Six years earlier in 1954, almost unnoticed on the strategic chess board of nuclear affairs, the French had lost a battle to guerillas at Dien Bien Phu, in Vietnam. This would set in motion other events that would soon challenge fundamentally, yet again, the strategic thinking of future presidents and future congresses.

Conclusion

Histories of the evolution of U.S. nuclear strategy and U.S. strategic capabilities consistently have overlooked the role of the Congress. This may partially account for why, even today, the executive branch and military services often underestimate the independence and importance of congressional perspectives and powers, with sometimes frustrating consequences for the executive's preferred strategic policies and military service strategic programs. Yet Congress has played an important and often crucial role in building the strategies and capabilities that are the U.S. strategic posture. Indeed, during the period 1942 to 1960, Congress was an indispensable and often dominant actor.

The Manhattan Project that developed the first atomic bombs, a vast scientific and industrial enterprise, unprecedented for its scale and secrecy, could not have succeeded without the active collaboration of key members of Congress.

In the immediate aftermath of World War II, Congress saved from dissolution the Manhattan Project's scientific-industrial base at Los Alamos, Argonne, Oak Ridge, Hanford and elsewhere; and expanded this base to meet the growing needs of the Cold War. Congress created new institutions, such as the Atomic Energy Commission, the Joint Committee on Atomic

Energy, the Department of Defense, the Joint Chiefs of Staff, the National Security Council, and the Central Intelligence Agency, which collectively, along with the Congress itself, provided the institutional framework that guided the development of U.S. strategic thinking. Congress, it is no exaggeration to say, laid the material and intellectual foundations upon which was built the U.S. strategic posture for decades to come, until the present time.

Congress saved the H-bomb project from being delayed or stopped. Congress was the driving force behind development of thermonuclear weapons and even established a new nuclear weapons laboratory at Lawrence Livermore for the purpose of accelerating the H-bomb.

Initially, Congress went along with Air Force plans to underfund and even neglect ICBM development. When the Soviet Union surprised the United States by demonstrating an ICBM capability in 1957, Congress and the nation were jolted awake by the idea that the Soviets would unilaterally possess long-range nuclear missiles, a military advantage that could have catastrophic consequences for the U.S. strategic posture. Congress became the chief proponent for ICBMs, overcoming a still resistant Air Force and an Eisenhower administration reluctant to acknowledge the strategic threat, to quickly achieve deployment of the first U.S. ICBMs in 1960.

Congress contributed significantly to the development of strategic thinking that became the basis for nuclear strategy and operational planning throughout the early Cold War. Congress contributed to intellectual fermentation among the Air Force, Navy, and Army about their roles in the atomic age as the services competed for budgetary and programmatic priority. Congress anticipated, supported, and made possible President Eisenhower's New Look, the quintessential strategic posture of the 1942-1960 era.

Time and resources have not permitted this paper to draw more than a sketch of the role of Congress in this important period in the development of the U.S. strategic posture. Much more could be done on the topics addressed here. Future researchers may want to explore the role of Congress in developing air and anti-missile defenses; and civil defense, which had been the focus of entire hearings; and, in some cases, the exclusive interest of entire subcommittees.

Also unexplored is the role of the American people in building the strategic posture. Histories of nuclear weapons and strategy, including this paper, focus on elites. Yet Congress, especially the House of Representatives, whose members are elected every two years, is always running for re-election, and as an institution is highly sensitive to popular opinion. Congress provided a forum for the "average American" to share their views about the A-bomb, the H-bomb, the ICBM, and what should be done. Congressional records are a goldmine of information on the people's threat perceptions and popular reflections on strategic matters in testimony from civic groups, church groups, women's groups, unions, medical associations, school teachers and other parties broadly representative of America. To my knowledge, no effort has been made to explore and analyze this information. Even cursory examination of the record suggests that many "average Americans" had a sophisticated understanding of the strategic issues of the day. But sophisticated or unsophisticated, the views of the American people mattered because their support, or opposition, defined the limits of the politically possible. Moreover, modern political and military elites in the White House, the Congress, and the services perhaps should be interested in the record of how elite strategic decisions effected popular perceptions and lives, as the whole purpose of the strategic posture was to protect and serve the people.

Endnotes

[1] Stephen I. Schwartz (editor), *Atomic Audit: The Costs and Consequences of U.S. Nuclear Weapons Since 1940* (Washington, D.C.: Brookings Institution Press, 1998), pp. 486-491.

[2] "Four Trillion Dollars and Counting," *Bulletin of the Atomic Scientists*, Vol. 51, No. 6 (November 1, 1995), p. 4.

[3] Richard Rhodes, *The Making of the Atomic Bomb* (New York: Simon and Schuster, 1986).

[4] Peter J. Westwick, "In The Beginning: The Origin of Nuclear Secrecy," *Bulletin of the Atomic Scientists*, Vol. 56, No. 6 (November/December 2000), p. 44.

[5] Rhodes, op. cit., p. 314.

[6] Westwick, op. cit., p. 44.

[7] Janice Harper, "Secrets Revealed, Revelations Concealed: A Secret City Confronts its Environmental Legacy of Weapons Production," *Anthropological Quarterly*, Vol. 80, No. 1 (Winter 2007), pp. 39-42, 45, 47.

[8] William Burr (editor), "The Atomic Bomb and the End of World War II: A Collection of Primary Sources," *The National Security Archive*, National Security Archive Electronic Briefing Book No. 162 (Washington, D.C.: August 5, 2005), p. 5.

[9] Leslie R. Groves, *Now It Can Be Told: The Story of the Manhattan Project* (New York: Harper and Brothers, 1962), pp. 362-363.

[10] Ibid.

[11] "The CIA's Secret Funding and the Constitution," *Yale Law Journal*, 84 Yale L.J. 608 (January 1975), pp. 21-22. U.S. Senate, Committee on Armed Services, *Hearings on the National Security Act*, 80th Congress, 1st Session (Washington, D.C.: 1947), Part 2, p. 623.

[12] Groves, op. cit., pp. 360-363.

[13] Op. cit., *Yale Law Journal*, p. 22. Rhodes, op. cit., p. 617. Groves, op. cit., p. 365.

[14] Rhodes, op. cit., pp. 424, 620.

[15] Ibid, p. 750. Westwick, op. cit., p. 44. Henry DeWolf Smyth, *Atomic Energy for Military Purposes: The Official Report on the Development of the Atomic Bomb Under the Auspices of the United States Government* (Washington, D.C.: July 1, 1945).

[16] Vannevar Bush, *Modern Arms and Free Men: A Discussion of the Role of Science in Preserving Democracy* (New York: Simon and Schuster, 1949), pp. 258-259.

[17] Rhodes, op. cit., p. 750.

[18] Hearings Before The Committee On Military Affairs, U.S. House of Representatives, *Atomic Energy*, 69th Congress, 1st Session, October 9 and 19, 1945 (Washington, D.C.: U.S. Government Printing Office, 1945).

[19] Ibid, p. 1.

[20] Ibid, pp. 3-5.

[21] Rhodes, op. cit., Chapter 1.

[22] *Atomic Energy*, op. cit., p. 6.

[23] Ibid, p. 9.

[24] Ibid, p. 11.

[25] Ibid, p. 16.

[26] Ibid, p. 19.

[27] Ibid, p. 31.

[28] Ibid, p. 10.

[29] Ibid, pp. 24-28.

[30] Ibid. p. 23.

[31] Ibid, p. 17.

[32] Hearings Before The Special Committee On Atomic Energy, U.S. Senate, *A Resolution Creating A Special Committee To Investigate Problems relating To The Development, Use, And Control Of Atomic Energy*, 79th Congress, 1st Session, November 27-30, December 3, 1945 (Washington, D.C.: Printed for the Special Committee on Atomic Energy), Part 1, p. 1.

[33] Ibid, pp. 31-69.

[34] Ibid, p. 52.

[35] Ibid, pp. 145-148.

[36] Ibid, p. 147.

[37] Hearings Before The Special Committee On Atomic Energy, U.S. Senate, *A Resolution Creating A Special Committee To Investigate Problems Relating To The Development, Use, And Control Of Atomic Energy*, 79th Congress, 1st Session, December 13, 14, 19, 20, 1945 (Washington, D.C.: Printed for the Special Committee on Atomic Energy), Part 3, pp. 364-366, 396.

[38] Ibid, p. 392.

[39] Hearings Before The Special Committee On Atomic Energy, U.S. Senate, *A Resolution Creating A Special Committee To Investigate Problems Relating To The Development, Use, And Control Of Atomic Energy*, 79th Congress, 1st Session, December 5, 6, 10, 12, 1945 (Washington, D.C.: Printed for the Special Committee on Atomic Energy), Part 2, pp. 187, 193.

[40] Ibid, p. 194.

[41] Hearings Before The Committee On Military Affairs, U.S. House of Representatives, *An Act For The Development And Control Of Atomic Energy*, 79th Congress, 2nd Session, June 11, 12, 26, 1946 (Washington, D.C.: Printed for the Committee on Military Affairs), p. 19 see "S. 1717 (M'MAHON BILL)."

[42] Ibid, pp. 13-14, 25.

[43] Ibid, p. 24.

[44] Hearings Before The Special Committee On Atomic Energy, U.S. Senate, *A Bill For The Development And Control Of Atomic Energy*, 79th Congress, 2nd Session, April 4, 8, 1946 (Washington, D.C.: Printed for the Special Committee on Atomic Energy), Part 5, pp. 497-525.

[45] Hearings Before The Special Committee On Atomic Energy, U.S. Senate, *A Bill For The Development And Control Of Atomic Energy*, 79th Congress, 2nd Session, February 18, 19, 27, 1945 (Washington, D.C.: Printed for the Special Committee on Atomic Energy), Part 4, p. 494.

[46] Ibid, p. 473.

[47] Ibid, pp. 481-482.

[48] Hearings Before The Committee On Naval Affairs, U.S. Senate, *Unification Of The Armed Forces*, 79th Congress, 2nd Session, April 30; May 1-3, 6-9; July 2, 3, 9-11, 1946 (Washington, D.C.: U.S. Government Printing Office, 1946). *National Security Act of 1947*, United States Code, Chapter 343, Statute 496, approved July 26, 1947.

[49] Ibid.

[50] Ibid, pp. 3-7.

[51] Ibid, p. 43.

[52] Hearings Before The Committee On Armed Services, U.S. Senate, *National Defense Establishment (Unification Of The Armed Services)*, 80th Congress, 1st Session, March 18, 20, 25-26; April 1-3, 1947 (Washington, D.C.: U.S. Government Printing Office, 1947), Part 1, p. 91.

[53] Ibid, p. 237.

[54] Ibid, pp. 311-312.

[55] Hearings Before The Committee On Armed Services, U.S. Senate, *National Defense Establishment (Unification Of the Armed Services)*, 80th Congress, 1st Session, April 30; May 2, 6, 7, 9, 1947 (Washington, D.C.: U.S. Government Printing Office, 1947), Part 3, pp. 491-492.

[56] Ibid, p. 526.

[57] *Unification Of The Armed Forces*, op. cit., see note 48 for full cite, p. 127.

[58] Ibid, p. 73.

[59] David. A. Rosenberg, "American Atomic Strategy and the Hydrogen Bomb Decision," *The Journal of American History*, Vol. 1, No. 66 (June 1979), pp. 62-87. David A. Rosenberg, "The Origins of Overkill: Nuclear Weapons and American Strategy, 1945-1960," *International Security*, Vol. 7, No. 4 (Spring 1983), pp. 3-71.

[60] Thomas A. Bailey, *A Diplomatic History of the American People* (New York: Appleton-Century-Crofts, 1958), p. 789.

[61] See for example the estimate by General Groves in the congressional hearing *Atomic Energy*, op. cit., p. 18.

[62] Bailey, op. cit., p. 813.

[63] John Pike, "B-47 Stratojet United States Nuclear Forces," *GlobalSecurity.org*, http://www.globalsecurity.org/wmd/systems/b-47.htm. .Rosenberg, op. cit., pp. 3-71.

[64] *National Defense Establishment*, op. cit., see note 55 for full cite, Part 3, p. 641.

[65] Bailey, op. cit., 796-797, 800-803.

[66] Rosenberg, op. cit., pp. 3-71. Lawrence Freedman, *The Evolution of Nuclear Strategy* (New York: St. Martin's Press, 1983), pp. 52-55.

[67] Hearings Before The Subcommittee Of The Committee On Appropriations, U.S. House of Representatives, *Military Functions, National Military Establishment Appropriation Bill For 1949*, 80th Congress, 2nd Session (Washington, D.C.: U.S. Government Printing Office, 1948), Part 2, p. 3.

[68] Ibid, p. 4.

[69] Hearings Before The Subcommittee Of The Committee On Appropriations, U.S. House of Representatives, *Military Functions, National Military Establishment Appropriation Bill For 1949*, 80th Congress, 2nd Session (Washington, D.C.: U.S. Government Printing Office, 1948), Part 3, p. 1.

[70] Ibid, p. 1222.

[71] Henry A. Kissinger, *Nuclear Weapons and Foreign Policy* (New York: Harper and Brothers, 1957), p. 35.

[72] Ibid, p. 35. Hearings Before The Committee On Armed Services, U.S. House of Representatives, *The National Defense Program--Unification and Strategy*, 81st Congress, 1st Session (Washington, D.C.: U.S. Government Printing Office, 1949), pp. 50-51.

[73] Bailey, op. cit., 789, 818-819.

[74] Hearings Before The Committee On Armed Services And The Committee On Foreign Relations, U.S. Senate, *Military Situation In The Far East*, 82nd Congress, 1st Session, June1,2, 4-9, 11-13, 1951 (Washington, D.C.: U.S. Government Printing Office, 1951), Part 3, pp. 1676-1679

[75] Ibid, pp. 2179-2180.

[76] Ibid, p. 2397.

[77] Ibid, p. 2398.

[78] Hearings Before The Committee On Armed Services And The Committee On Foreign Relations, U.S. Senate, *Military Situation In The Far East*, 82nd Congress, 1st Session, June 14, 15, 18-22, 25, 27, 1951 (Washington, D.C.: U.S. Government Printing Office, 1951), Part 4, p. 3074.

[79] *Military Situation In The Far East*, op. cit., Part 3, pp. 2484-2485.

[80] Ibid, pp. 220-221.

[81] *Military Situation In The Far East*, op. cit. Part 4, p. 2588.

[82] See for example Albert J. Wohlstetter, *Selection and Use of Strategic Air Bases*, R-266 (RAND Corp.: April 1954).

[83] James R. Killian (Chairman), Technological Capabilities Panel, *Meeting the Threat of Surprise Attack* (Washington, D.C.: Department of Defense, February 1955).

[84] Hearings Before The Subcommittee On The Air Force Of The Committee On Armed Services, U.S. Senate, *Study Of Airpower*, 84th Congress, 2nd Session, April 25-27, 30, and May 2, 1956 (Washington, D.C.: U.S. Government Printing Office, 1956), Part 2, p. 161.

[85] Ibid, p. 102.

[86] Hearings Before The Subcommittee On The Air Force Of The Committee On Armed Services, U.S. Senate, *Study Of Airpower*, 84th Congress, 2nd session, April 16, 20, 1956 (Washington, D.C.: U.S. Government Printing Office, 1956), Part I, p. 39.

[87] Hearings Before The Subcommittee On The Air Force Of The Committee On Armed Services, U.S. Senate, *Study Of Airpower*, 84th Congress, 2nd Session, June 18, 27, 1956 (Washington, D.C.: U.S. Government Printing Office, 1956), Part XVIII, pp. 1340, 1341, 1363.

[88] Hearings Before The Subcommittee On The Air Force Of The Committee On Armed Services, U.S. Senate, *Study Of Airpower*, 84th Congress, 2nd Session, June 18, 25, 1956 (Washington, D.C.: U.S. Government Printing Office, 1956), Part XVII, pp. 1271-1272.

[89] *Study Of Airpower*, op. cit., Part 2, p. 161.

[90] Hearings Before The Subcommittee On The Air Force Of The Committee On Armed Services, U.S. Senate, *Study Of Airpower*, 84th Congress, 2nd Session, June 6, 7, 13, 1956 (Washington, D.C.: U.S. Government Printing Office, 1956), Part XII, pp. 997-998.

[91] Hearings Before The Subcommittee On The Air Force Of The Committee On Armed Services, U.S. Senate, *Study Of Airpower*, 84th Congress, 2nd Session, July 19, 1956 (Washington, D.C.: U.S. Government Printing Office, 1956), Part XXIII, pp. 1849-1850.

[92] Hearings Before The Subcommittee On The Air Force Of The Committee On Armed Services, U.S. Senate, *Study Of Airpower*, 84th Congress, 2nd Session, June 14, 1956 (Washington, D.C.: U.S. Government Printing Office, 1956), Part XIII, P. 1117.

[93] Hearings Before The Joint Committee On Atomic Energy, Untitled (Washington, D.C.: month/day indistinct on best copy, 1950), p. 2.

[94] Ibid, pp. 6-11, 16-19.

[95] Hearings Before The Joint Committee On Atomic Energy, *Development Of A Superweapon* (Washington, D.C.: January 9, 1950), pp. 17, 20-22.

[96] Ibid, p. 23.

[97] Ibid, p. 3.

[98] Ibid, pp. 35-41.

[99] Hearings Before The Joint Committee On Atomic Energy, *Discussion Of The Supplemental Budget, Fuchs Case, British Mission, Joan Hinton Case, Hydrogen Bomb Development* (Washington, D.C.: February 10, 1950), p. 534.

[100] Ibid, pp. 531-532, 542, 552-553, 539-540.

[101] Hearings Before The Joint Committee On Atomic Energy, *Developments In The Hydrogen Bomb* (Washington, D.C.: March 10, 1950), p. 13.

[102] Ibid, pp. 26-27.

[103] Ibid, pp. 39-40.

[104] Hearings Before The Joint Committee On Atomic Energy, *H-Bomb Development* (Washington, D.C.: March 28, 1950), p. 292.

[105] Ibid, pp. 263-264, 270-271, 291-293.

[106] Hearings Before The Joint Committee On Atomic Energy, *Dr. Hans Bethe* (Washington, D.C.: May 3, 1950), pp. 1-20, passim.

[107] Ibid, p. 16.

[108] Hearings Before The Joint Committee On Atomic Energy, *H-Bomb Status Report* (Washington, D.C.: September 28, 1951), pp. 1909, 1929-1934.

[109] Ibid, p. 1937.

[110] Hearings Before The Joint Committee On Atomic Energy, *Status Of Hydrogen Project* (Washington, D.C.: February 21, 1952), pp. 1-3, passim.

[111] "Ivy-Mike Nuclear Test," *Nucleasrfiles.org*, http://www.nuclearfiles.org/menu/key-issues/nuclear-weapons/issues/testing/test-ivy-mike.h.

[112] "The Soviet Nuclear Weapon Program," *Nuclearweaponarchive.org*, http://nuclearweaponarchive.org/Russia/Sovwpnprog.html, p. 4.

[113] *Meeting the Threat of Surprise Attack*, op. cit, for full citation see note 83.

[114] The Gaither Report: Security Resources Panel of the Scientific Advisory Committee, *Deterrence and Survival in the Nuclear Age* (Washington, D.C.: November 1957) declassified January 1973.

[115] Hearings Before The Preparedness Investigating Subcommittee Of The Committee On Armed Services, United States Senate, *Inquiry Into Satellite And Missile Programs*, 85th Congress, 2nd Session, November 25-27, December 13-14, 16-17, 1957 and January 10, 13, 15-17, 20-23, 1958 (Washington, D.C.: U.S. Government Printing Office, 1958), Part I, p. 59.

[116] U.S. War Department, *The United States Strategic Bombing Survey: Summary Report (European War)* (Washington, D.C.: February 30, 1945).

[117] Quoted in: Edmund Beard, *Developing the ICBM: A Study in Bureaucratic Politics* (New York: Columbia University Press, 1976), pp. 69-70. See also *Inquiry Into Satellite and Missile Programs*, op. cit., p. 823.

[118] Still the definitive work on military service bureaucratic rivalry over ICBM development is Beard, op. cit., full citation in note 117.

[119] *Military Functions, National Military Establishment Appropriation Bill For 1949*, op. cit., for full citation see note 67, p. 145.

[120] Hearings Before The Subcommittee On The Air Force Of The Committee On Armed Services, U.S. Senate, *Study Of Airpower*, 84th Congress, 2nd Session (Washington, D.C.: U.S. Government Printing Office, 1956), Part VIII, p. 614; Part IX, p. 775; Part XIII; XIV, p. 43.

[121] For full citation of the congressional hearings *Inquiry Into Satellite And Missile Programs* see note 115.

[122] *Inquiry Into Satellite And Missile Programs*, op. cit. pp. 1-3.

[123] Ibid, pp. 475-476, 642.

[124] Ibid, pp. 907, 906-913.

[125] Ibid, p. 840.

[126] Ibid, pp. 901-902.

[127] Ibid, pp. 844-845.

[128] Freedman, op. cit., pp. 414-415, note 9.

[129] *Inquiry Into Satellite And Missile Programs*, op. cit., pp. 198-199.

[130] Ibid, p. 243.

[131] Ibid, p. 195, 196.

[132] Ibid, pp. 231-232.

[133] Ibid, p. 232.

[134] David Alan Rosenberg, "A Smoking Radiating Ruin at the End of Two Hours: Documents on American War Plans for Nuclear War with the Soviet Union 1954-55," *International Security*, Vol. 6, No. 3 (Winter 1981/82). Rosenberg, "The Origins of Overkill," op. cit., full citation note 59.

[135] The Harmon Report, *Evaluation of the Effect on Soviet War Effort Resulting from the Strategic Air Offensive* (May 11, 1949) reprinted in Thomas H. Etzold and John Lewis Gaddis, *Containment: Documents on American Policy and Strategy 1945-1950* (New York: Columbia University Press, 1968).

[136] Joint Chiefs of Staff, *DROPSHOT* (1949) reprinted in Anthony Cave Brown (editor), *DROPSHOT: The American Plan for World War III Against Russia in 1957* (New York: Dial Press, 1978).

[137] Fred Kaplan, *The Wizards of Armageddon* (New York: Simon and Schuster, 1983), pp. 181-182.

[138] Ibid, p. 182.

[139] Ibid, p. 183.

[140] National Security Council, *NSC 68: United States Objectives and Programs of National Security* (Washington, D.C.: April 14, 1950).

[141] Freedman, op. cit. pp. 84-85.

[142] National Security Council, *Basic National Security Policy*, NSC-162/2 (Washington, D.C.: October 30, 1955) and quoted in Freedman, op. cit, pp. 81-82.

[143] John Foster Dulles, "The Evolution of Foreign Policy," *Department of State Bulletin* (Washington, D.C.: January 25, 1954), pp. 107-110 (original emphasis). See also Kaplan, op. cit. p. 175.

[144] Hearings Before The Special Committee on Atomic Energy, op. cit., for full citation see note 37, Part 3, pp. 364, 392.

[145] Ibid, p. 394.

[146] Ibid, p. 395-396.

[147] Hearings Before The Subcommittee Of The Committee On Appropriations, op. cit., for full citation see note 69, Part 3, pp. 5-6.

[148] Hearings Before The Joint Committee On Atomic Energy, Untitled (Washington, D.C.: May 13, 1950), pp. 1-7.

[149] Ibid, p. 7.

[150] *Developments In The Hydrogen Bomb*, op. cit., for full citation see note 101, pp. 13.

[151] *H-Bomb Status Report*, op. cit., p. 1937.

[152] Hearings Before The Subcommittee On The Air Force Of The Committee On Armed Services, *Study Of Airpower*, 84th Congress, 2nd Session (Washington, D.C.: 1956), Part IX, pp. 705-775; Part X, pp. 832; Part XI, p. 894; Part XVII, pp. 1271-1273.

www.ingramcontent.com/pod-product-compliance
Lightning Source LLC
Chambersburg PA
CBHW081853280526
45789CB00007B/2678